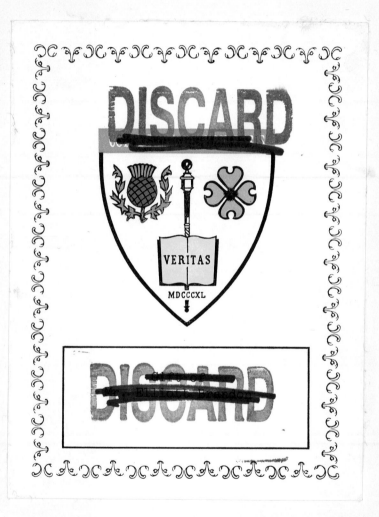

FREDERIC BASTIAT

A Man Alone

Frédéric Bastiat

ARCHITECTS OF FREEDOM SERIES

FREDERIC BASTIAT

A Man Alone

GEORGE CHARLES ROCHE III

ARLINGTON HOUSE   *New Rochelle, N.Y.*

Library of Congress Catalog Card Number 71-139891
ISBN 0-87000-116-7

MANUFACTURED IN THE UNITED STATES OF AMERICA

To JUNE,
who knows so much more French than her husband.

Contents

10

Foreword

WHEN FOLLOWING THE IDEAS OF FREDERIC BASTIAT, THE
reader often wishes to know a bit more about the man himself.
This applies to many thinkers of consequence—we find their
ideas so interesting that we think their lives must be equally
exciting and significant. Bastiat, however, has remained a shad-
owy entity, even to his few biographers. The same scant details
of the man's personal life appear in each of the several sketches
devoted to his career.

In Bastiat's case, it appears that there is little to tell concerning most of his personal life. Bastiat apparently spent his first
45 years in quiet preparation for the enormous flash of productive activity which occurred during his last five years.

Certainly the best study of Bastiat's life is the most recent—
Professor Dean Russell's doctoral dissertation—later revised
into book form, *Frederic Bastiat: Ideas and Influence.* Professor Russell emphasized the political significance of Bastiat's
thought rather more than previous studies had done, thus directing attention to a main thrust of the man's life. However,
a fully rounded picture of Bastiat can be developed only if we
view his age in historical perspective.

To see Bastiat's significance clearly, it is necessary to study him as more than an economic journalist; more, even, than a political theorist. Bastiat must be analyzed against the historical background which molded his time: the Revolutions of 1789, 1830, and 1848, together with the forces generated by the Industrial Revolution and the response to those forces, especially in England and France. For in that upheaval and in Bastiat's response to it, we find awaiting us an improved understanding of the middle-class political revolution which has dominated the Western world ever since. In Bastiat's analysis of French politics, in his relation to the English Whig tradition, in the contrasting political and social thought as expressed by Bastiat and some of his contemporaries, notably Alexis de Tocqueville, we find new insights into the conservative-libertarian makeup that have a great deal of relevance for our own ideologically confused age.

Acknowledgement is due all those who previously have examined aspects of Bastiat's life and thought, particularly Professor Russell. My editor and good friend at Arlington House, Llewellyn Rockwell, provided consistent encouragement from start to finish. The Foundation for Economic Education staff also did much to make this book possible. Mrs. Muriel Brown freely gave of both her secretarial assistance and her unbounded enthusiasm. Edmund Opitz provided several very helpful lines of thought which greatly improved my own understanding of Bastiat, while Paul Poirot generously provided his customary patience, insight, and good sense during all phases of the manuscript's preparation. Special thanks also go to Leonard Read, who years ago rescued Bastiat from the historical ash-heap and who was among the first to realize the enormous importance of Frederic Bastiat.

Introduction

FOR THE PAST TWO CENTURIES, THE WESTERN WORLD HAS been torn by a continuing debate: Does the well-being of society as a whole stem from the freedom of enlightened individuals to pursue their own interests; or must government intervene in the lives of its citizens to assure the greatest collective good? Oddly enough, the liberal historically has taken first one side and then the other in that debate. "Liberal" today implies a readiness to use government as a problem-solving device, as a handy and absolutely necessary tool to save the citizens of the republic from the dangerous effects of excessive freedom. In the first half of the nineteenth century, during the lifetime of Frederic Bastiat, "liberal" had a precisely opposite meaning. For Bastiat and the liberals of his age, the encroachment of the state in the lives of its citizens was not a solution to society's problems, but instead was the problem itself.

Though the meaning of the word "liberal" has changed greatly since Bastiat's day, the underlying argument has not. We are still trying to decide whether or not government should be the final arbiter of men's lives. This is why Bastiat's words have so much relevance today. He addresses himself to the central argument of our own times. And he does so in a fashion as down-to-earth as our daily lives. Always quick to defend the consumer, the forgotten little men of most modern economic analyses, Bastiat writes in terms at once understandable and entertaining. He often turns a withering blast of ridicule on those who presume to know what's best for everyone else. And, of course, to be laughed at is the one thing which big government has never been able to stand.

Writing long before government reached the enormous proportions of our own times, Bastiat predicted the history of the past century:

> The state quickly understands the use it can make of the role the public entrusts to it. It will be the arbiter, the master of all destinies. It will take a great deal; hence, a great deal will remain for itself. It will multiply the number of its agents; it will enlarge the scope of its prerogatives; it will end by acquiring overwhelming proportions.

Few of today's readers will even recognize the name of Frederic Bastiat. Yet he was one of those men fated to stand at the crossroads of sweeping historical events and radically conflicting ideologies. He lived his life in the turbulent aftermath of the French Revolution and personally witnessed the upheavals of 1830 and 1848. He was active in the political and ideological debates of his age. The battles he fought as a mid–nineteenth-century public figure were the battles which still mold the events and the thinking of the Western world. This perhaps explains the timely and lively quality of Bastiat's thinking which immediately strikes the reader of today.

As an author, columnist, and politician during a stormy period of French history which brought the citizens to the barricades again and again and which witnessed the overthrow of several French governments, Bastiat realized that the radical changes induced by the Industrial Revolution were making a totally new society of Europe. There could be no road back to the past, no staying the hand of change. He saw before most of his contemporaries that Western men had their destinies in their own hands as never before. Prosperity or disaster awaited the new industrial world, depending upon a single issue: would men allow the system to work, or would they, in Bastiat's phrase, "fear liberty" too much to give themselves this new beginning? Bastiat realized that the very complexity of the new order demanded a flexibility that the dead hand of government planning could not tolerate, a flexibility which only individual freedom in transactions could supply. The slender Frenchman spent his life fighting to give all Frenchmen the freedom which alone could make the specialized world of the Industrial Revolution function properly.

Socialists, communists, visionaries, demagogues, and planners of every description were all his foes. He stood steadfastly and often alone against the trend of his time. Even such allies as he had in the struggle were not always in agreement with him. True, Bastiat and his thought were related to Burke, Mill, and the Whig tradition in England. True, Bastiat joined Alexis de Tocqueville in his resistance to the influences of the French Revolution. It is even true that in many ways Bastiat drew heavily on the thought which typified the nineteenth century. Yet, somehow Bastiat was a man alone, not only in his lofty independence, but also in the frank and fearless application of his ideas. The search for popularity and approval never shifted him from his chosen course. Perhaps this is why Bastiat speaks so clearly to us today: His vision was unclouded by the rhetoric of his age.

No doubt his unqualified insistence upon individual liberty limited his influence during his own lifetime, but it is precisely that same insistence which makes Frederic Bastiat so important to those of us living in another age which has largely lost its way in a series of authoritarian blind alleys.

CHAPTER 1

A Time of Preparation

He is as good as he is lazy. If he is going to do something in life, he is going to have to change radically.

IN THE SOUTH OF FRANCE THE ROLLING GREEN HILLS ARE carefully kept by a frugal people. As those hills roll to the extreme southwestern tip of French soil, the gentle pastoral nature of the countryside is suddenly interrupted by the grim outline of the Pyrenees. Beneath the shadow of the mountains, on the shore of the Bay of Biscay, Claude Frederic Bastiat was born in 1801, on a warm June day in the small provincial town of Bayonne. Pierre Bastiat, Frederic's father, was a prominent merchant in the community.

The boy's mother died in 1808. The merchant then left Bayonne to move northward to an even smaller provincial town, Mugron. Perhaps he made the move inland in quest of drier air, since he suffered from a weak chest and had not been able to gain lasting physical strength, despite visits to a number of health resorts.

Soon after his mother's death, the seven-year-old boy traveled to his new home with his ailing father. The town of Mugron was located in the valley of the Adour River, where the Bastiat estate had previously belonged to the Marquis of

Poyanne. The Bastiat family had acquired the property after the Revolution. The estate was small, but well kept, and the little family soon settled into a new routine of quiet country living. Pierre Bastiat doted on the boy and found him a great comfort after the death of his wife. He thought the boy had real ability, but wondered what the youngster might do with his life:

> He is as good as he is lazy. If he is going to do something in life, he is going to have to change radically. Frederic is always pleasant and good natured; but he has a lazy streak that is without equal.

> Frederic is an angel, with such gaiety, such spirit, and a sweetness beyond compare. What a shame that I don't have the means to give him the education that he deserves. He is a charming child, always happy and singing; I've never seen him to be capricious. I hope he will live up to my expectations.

Whatever those expectations, Pierre Bastiat was not to see them fulfilled. He died in 1810, leaving young Frederic orphaned. The boy was taken in by his paternal grandfather and his maiden aunt. Justine Bastiat, his aunt, was rather a forceful old lady, said to possess the prominent nose of the Bastiat men. She and everyone around her did as she pleased, and she was much given to evenings at cards with her spinster friends. Despite her formidable exterior, the old woman was sincerely interested in young Frederic and between them there grew a lasting bond of affection.

In a Bayonne school presided over by Father Meillan, Frederic had already acquired the beginnings of his 3Rs, together with a sound basis in Christian doctrine. Aunt Justine soon concerned herself with his formal education and enrolled him in Saint-Sever, but was disappointed with the school's quality. Bastiat then was enrolled at the Benedictine college of Sorèze, which had a far superior reputation. It was here that he developed such a great taste for reading and here that he acquired the knowledge of English which was to play so large a role in forming his close ties with the English and American concepts of free trade and freedom in transactions.

It was here that Bastiat found a close friend in M. V. Calmètes. The two young men often studied together and in 1818 won a gold medal for a poem on which they had collaborated. Something of young Frederic's loneliness can perhaps be detected in his statement to his friend when they won the medal: "Keep it. I am an orphan; you have both father and mother, and the medal of right falls to them." That loneliness may well be the reason that Bastiat and Calmètes were so close. Though Bastiat was an active and fairly rugged young man, at school he turned toward an introspective and quiet way of life, at least in part because Calmètes was not healthy enough to keep up a more vigorous physical pace.

Though Calmètes completed his studies at Sorèze and went on to be a lawyer, Bastiat did not stay at school long enough to graduate. At 17, he left Sorèze and went to work for his uncle in Bayonne, in the same firm where his father had previously been a partner. Having failed to complete his own baccalaureat degree, Bastiat remained hostile to the whole degree system of higher education for the rest of his life. Indeed, his first published essay, years later, was on the necessity for reforms in French education.

Bayonne

In his uncle's counting house, it soon became apparent that young Bastiat was not well suited to a career as a merchant. His habits of quiet study and wide-ranging reading stayed with him in the business world, and he seemed more at home with literature than with ledgers. Devoted to French, English, and Italian literature, the 19-year-old Bastiat described his ambition as ". . . nothing less than to become acquainted with politics, history, geography, mathematics, mechanics, natural history, botany, and four or five languages."

In a letter to his friend Calmètes in the spring of 1820, the quiet, studious youngster admitted, "I entered the world step by step, but I didn't burst into it." This world of Bayonne into which he entered was an exciting, intellectual center for a provincial town. Not all French intellectual life was centered in Paris. Voltaire and Rousseau were both influential among men of ideas, and it was during this period that Bastiat had his youthful fling with religious skepticism. When his cousin entered the priesthood, Bastiat wrote his friend, "This bringing together of God and of men, this Redemption. How nice it must be to believe in it! What an invention, Calmètes, if it is one!" The skepticism was short-lived and Bastiat soon returned to the traditional Catholic faith.

Affairs at his uncle's counting house sometimes attracted Frederic's attention. The Napoleonic Wars had ravaged French ports like Bayonne for two decades; controls of all sorts had set back Bayonne's commerce to a point well below its eighteenth-century levels. Even after 1815, controls of the French government were proving nearly as restrictive as the English blockade had ever been. For young Frederic, this first-hand experience was convincing proof that the economic affairs of citizens always suffered when they became objects of public policy. The solution? Economic prosperity demanded economic liberty—men must be freed from the deadly hand of government control.

Observation of the hard times which had fallen upon Bayonne first turned Bastiat to serious study of political economy, especially the works of Jean-Baptiste Say and Adam Smith. Many of the ideas of a free economic order had been foreshadowed in the eighteenth-century work of the Physiocrats, especially Francois Quesnay. In fact, Adam Smith had known Quesnay and acknowledged a substantial debt to him when *Wealth of Nations* was published in 1776. Smith in turn had greatly influenced Say, whose book *Traite d'economie politique* proved so exciting and provocative for the young Bastiat. In a letter to Calmetes, Frederic described his triumph in a debate before a Bayonne discussion group of which he was a member, attributing his success to using Say's free market arguments. From that time on, Bastiat devoured the ideas on freedom which had been developing in France, England, and America for the past century.

Mugron

By 1824, the budding young intellectual had no desire whatsoever to stay on in his uncle's business. He dreamed of going to Paris to pursue formal studies. At this point, his old and ill grandfather asked him to return to Mugron, to the area where he had lived for a time before Pierre Bastiat's death. For the second time in his life, Frederic Bastiat suppressed his taste for an active, outgoing life out of regard for someone close to him. Once before, at school, he had turned to the quiet, introspective pursuits best suited to his friend, Calmètes. Now he again found himself following the same path, this time for love of his grandfather: "I am putting aside all ambitious projects and am returning again to my solitary studies." Thus, in his 23rd year, Bastiat found himself in the serene countryside of the Bastiat family estate, a retreat where he was destined to spend the next 20 years of his life in quiet study.

The elder Bastiat died the next year, leaving his estate to the 24-year-old Frederic. Perhaps influenced by the Physiocrats, who had been steeped in agrarian attitudes, Bastiat at once undertook to revolutionize farming practices not only on his own estate, but through the entire area of the Adour River Valley. He attempted to establish a local learned society on the Physiocratic model, specializing in both agricultural and economic studies. A few months of effort to modernize agricultural practices and propagate liberal economic ideas among his provincial neighbors soon discouraged the young man, who was heard to comment, "What would you have if you had a philharmonic society composed of the deaf?"

Bastiat fared little better in introducing new agricultural practices on his own estate, where he had a dozen tenant farmers. Whatever notions the young man had of scientific agriculture, he lacked the business ability to keep the necessary detailed records and lacked the firmness to defend his own interests. He was so easily dissuaded from his reforms that the only beneficiaries were the tenants, never the landlord himself. "Scientific agriculture" soon came to nothing, and life on the Bastiat estate settled into a peaceful round of solitude and scholarship. Bastiat readily admitted that he cared little for money and less for business, preferring, as he said in one of his letters, not to undergo irksome labor for three-fourths of his life merely to ensure a useless superfluity for the remainder. Books and ideas were to be his life, and a happy enough life it was, except for the "short-lived melancholy" described by one of his biographers.

An event calculated to end any melancholy in Bastiat's life occurred soon after he returned to Mugron. Felix Coudroy, a brilliant young intellectual who lived on a neighboring estate, soon became a close friend, thus providing the conversation and stimulation which played such an important role in rounding out Bastiat's development.

These two men who were destined to find so much in common were quite unlike in both temperament and viewpoint. Coudroy was a recent graduate of the law school in Toulouse. Deeply steeped in Rousseau, he was frankly socialistic and authoritarian, believing that no lasting social order was possible unless all individual wills were subjugated to a central authority. To Coudroy, any discussion of freedom and individuality implied anarchy and the collapse of the social order.

To the liberal young Bastiat, deeply read in Adam Smith and J. B. Say, Coudroy was a challenging specimen of everything wrong with nineteenth-century French thought. Again and again the two young friends met to argue the place of self-interest, the role of a free market, the necessity for individual dignity. In the end, Bastiat converted Coudroy to the liberal view, and in the process refined and strengthened his own understanding. In this one-to-one relationship, some genuine teaching had taken place, and both teacher and taught were better for the exchange.

For the next 20 years, these two men studied and conversed on a daily basis. Coudroy was more plodding and methodical, Bastiat more mercurial and intuitive. In the endless parade of books they devoured, each volume would more likely be read first in its entirety by Coudroy, who would mark the key passages for Bastiat. Only when a book interested him deeply would Bastiat read it completely. All the reading and thinking of the two men would then be subjected to careful, analytical conversation. In this fashion, philosophy, religion, history, political theory, biography—works of every description—helped form a part of the thought of Frederic Bastiat. Surely even

Bastiat could not have suspected that this lifetime of work was being stored against a day, when in the face of terrible pressures and illness, this slender, shy Frenchman would pour forth an enormous amount of published work at a critical moment in French history. Perhaps one of the best-kept secrets of all famous men (kept even from the men themselves) is the extent to which destiny prepares those from whom great things are expected.

For a time it seemed that Bastiat would interrupt his life of intensive study to take a wife. In his late 20's, he had written, "I would like a wife . . . I can't picture her, but I sense it more than I am able to express it. I shall be the teacher of my children. They shall not be brought up like those in the village, nor like savages in the desert." But destiny had other plans once again. When nearly 30, he married Marie Hiard, a young local girl. "However," in the words of one French biographer, "he adopted the wrong procedure for becoming a father since he left the church after the ceremony. The marriage was at the insistence of her family. Just an innocent affair."

Bastiat had thus lived through marriage, one major event which greatly changes the lives of most men, and yet had suffered no visible effect on his way of life. He was about to face another upheaval which would disturb the life of all France.

CHAPTER 2

Revolution: 1830

> I waited for the blood, but the only thing that poured out was wine. This evening we fraternized with the officers of the garrison. Punch, wine, liquors, and especially the songs of Beranger added zest to the party.

THE FRENCH REVOLUTION, WHICH HAD BEGUN IN 1789 AS an experiment in "popular" rule, brought a decade of unparalleled chaos and suffering to the people of France. The nation was "saved" from its sad fate by the inevitable dictator. Such men always seem to arrive following the total collapse of a social order. In 1799, the dictator's name was Napoleon Bonaparte. The years of Bastiat's childhood were marked by the military adventurism and authoritarian rule of the Napoleonic regime. The chaos of the revolutionary regime, followed by the endless wars of the Napoleonic regime, offered little real difference to the French people.

By 1815, the average Frenchman probably wondered what purpose the past 25 years of suffering had served. After all, the Revolution had begun with the effort to rid France of Bourbon rule. Thus the appointment between Madam Guillotine and Louis XVI. Yet, after the Treaty of Paris ended the Napoleonic era, the French found themselves with another Bourbon on the throne. The Restoration had placed Louis XVIII, brother of the beheaded French king, in his "rightful" position as ruler of France.

Louis XVIII also brought a return to many of the pre-revolutionary aristocratic privileges of property and class. The clergy promptly reinstated its authority over the 70% of the French population which composed the peasantry. The French peasant had never understood what was happening in Paris, and had tended to accept the turmoil and hardship of revolution and dictatorship as events on a par with bad weather: completely beyond control or comprehension, and therefore to be borne with a shrug. To such men, it must have seemed that revolution had indeed brought more hardship than change to France.

It has been said of the Bourbons that they had learned nothing and had forgotten nothing, implying that the monarchy after 1815 had ignored everything which had occurred for the past 25 years. Yet there were changes. A large part of the Revolutionary land settlements (including the land comprising the Bastiat estate) were retained in force. It is also true that, while the king retained executive authority, the new constitution limited royal power by calling for a two-house legislature with full authority to make the laws. In practice, however, the life of the typical Frenchman was little changed—a constant round of exertions to keep ahead of the tax collector. Whether the taxes were collected in the name of "the people" or "the king" made little practical difference.

Louis XVIII died in 1824, the year that young Frederic Bastiat returned to his estate in Mugron. But if Bastiat or any other Frenchman expected greater freedom after the old man's passing, he was sorely mistaken. Charles X, yet *another* brother of Louis XVI, mounted the throne and began an even more enthusiastically repressive regime.

Charles X began talking publicly of "the divine right of kings." He proposed that all nobles should be indemnified at state expense for property lost in the Revolution. He demanded that all books and newspapers sold in France must first gain the approval of a committee appointed by the king. In short, he did everything possible to antagonize Frenchmen. Poor, tired France, willing to accept almost any indignity and interference in order to procure a few years of stability! But Charles X was too much even for revolution-weary Frenchmen.

In the legislative elections of 1830, Charles was completely repudiated. A wiser man might have heeded the warning; but not Charles X. On the morning of July 26, he attempted a coup d'etat, dissolving the new legislature and abolishing all freedom to discuss the royal authority. The French, who by this time had developed a certain skill and confidence in revolutionary technique, rose up in the famous July days—27, 28, and 29— and made it clear that the royal services of Charles X were no longer required. In the *Devil's Dictionary*, Ambrose Bierce defines abdication as: "An act whereby a sovereign attests his sense of the high temperature of the throne." Charles X so attested at the end of July 1830, departing for England.

The bourgeoisie all over France celebrated his departure. Bastiat had listened with increasing uneasiness for the past two years as the petty nobility in the vicinity of Mugron had approvingly discussed a return to absolutism and the benefits likely to accrue to them as the result. As Bastiat neared thirty, he became increasingly convinced that some form of constitutional government, based upon solid bourgeois foundations, was absolutely necessary for France. Members of the French middle class, largely excluded from suffrage in the Restoration

period, were ready to sing the praises of "democracy," since the
word to them meant the transfer of power from the nobility to
the bourgeoisie.

Not all those who opposed Charles X and his policies were
so assured that the bourgeois rule would answer all problems.
A young man of Bastiat's generation, Alexis de Tocqueville,
had also studied the course of events since 1789. He saw the
whole era as a struggle to the death between France's nobility
and her middle class. In his view, the nobility was attempting
to retain control of French life, in a futile effort to resist the
rising power of the bourgeoisie. Tocqueville was to be proven
quite right. Later, in his *Récollections,* he could write:

> In 1830 the triumph of the middle class had been definite and so
> thorough that all political power, every franchise, every prerogative,
> and the whole government was confined and, as it were, heaped up
> within the narrow limits of this one class, to the statutory exclusion
> of all beneath them and the actual exclusion of all above. Not only
> did it thus rule society, but it may be said to have formed it. It
> entrenched itself in every vacant place, prodigiously augmented the
> number of places and accustomed itself to live almost as much upon
> the Treasury as upon its own industry.

The middle class had long complained of the abuses of political power perpetrated by the French nobility. Now the middle
class had taken political power unto itself. It remained to be
proven that political power was safer in the hands of its new
owners.

A Peaceful Revolutionary

The excitement of the July Days in Paris quickly penetrated the
provinces. Bastiat journeyed to Bayonne to join the revolutionary forces. The city of Bayonne had proclaimed itself in sup-

port of a change in government, and only the citadel of the city continued to fly the flag of the Bourbons. Rumors were also flying: perhaps Spanish troops were massing a few miles away at the frontier; perhaps the troops in the citadel were preparing to take over the city.

Bastiat revealed himself a true Frenchman in the crisis. He and his friends prepared a proclamation and formed an association of some 600, who promptly declared themselves willing to take the government citadel by force if necessary.

Instead, the citadel opened its gates. The officers of the garrison invited the young revolutionaries in to join a celebration. As Bastiat described it: "I waited for the blood, but the only thing that poured out was wine. This evening we fraternized with the officers of the garrison. Punch, wine, liquors, and especially the songs of Beranger added zest to the party."

So ended the military career of Frederic Bastiat, who soon returned to Mugron and his peaceful studies.

The Citizen King

The Revolution of 1830 was largely the work of the Parisian middle class. The bourgeoisie did not wish too radical a departure in French political life, preferring that the idea of a king be retained and asking only that the king be properly responsive to middle-class interests. How to achieve this delicate Gallic balance between change and continuity? The solution of this problem was the work of an old French hero, Lafayette. Now an old man, but still possessing enormous prestige with the French people, he was made head of the National Guard during the July Days. All eyes turned to this symbol of authority and integrity. For a time, Lafayette might have imposed any government he chose.

Some Frenchmen desired a republic; others, like the wily
Guizot and Thiers, favored middle-class power masked by
monarchy. Acceding to their advice, Lafayette threw his support to Louis Philippe. Cousin of the Bourbons, a member of
the Orleans family, Louis' credentials as royalty were in good
order. Equally important, Louis Philippe was willing to view
himself as the "Citizen King" and to serve as representative of
the wealthier bourgeoisie. The new sovereign discarded royal
robes, underplayed all pomp and ceremony, and posed as monarch by will of the people.

Like most of his contemporaries, Bastiat was solidly in favor
of the new middle-class regime. He considered that France's
troubles had originated in the prohibitive old regime of the
Bourbons and looked to a reign of economic and political
liberty under the wise government of the bourgeoisie. Parliamentary monarchy was all to the good now that the elite of the
French nation, the enlightened bourgeoisie, occupied the seats
of power. With the pear-shaped figure of Louis Philippe to
symbolize the new order of prosperity and stability, middle-
class France settled back with a sigh of satisfaction. Though the
current of revolution had begun in France, its reverberations
were more lasting among some of its neighbors, notably Belgium, Italy, and Germany. But for the French, the Revolution
of 1830 was over almost as quickly as it had begun.

The "Citizen King" and the new bourgeois order which he
epitomized are clearly presented in Tocqueville's memoirs.
Basing his writing upon his own observations in the Paris of the
1830's, he described Louis Philippe:

> Though he came from one of the noblest families in Europe, he
> concealed all hereditary pride deeply in his soul; nevertheless he
> certainly believed that there was no other human being like him. All

the same he had most of the qualities and defects which belong more particularly to the subaltern orders of society. He had regular habits and wanted those around him to have them too. He was orderly in his conduct, simple in his habits, his tastes were tempered; he was a born friend of the law, an enemy of all excesses, sober in his ways except in his desires. He was human without being sentimental, greedy and soft. He had no flaming passions, no ruinous weaknesses, no striking vices, and only one kingly virtue: courage. He was extremely polite, but without choice or greatness, a politeness of a merchant rather than of a Prince. He hardly appreciated literature or art, but he passionately loved industry. His memory was prodigious and capable of keeping the minutest detail. His conversation was prolix, diffuse, original and trivial, anecdotal, full of small facts, of salt and meaning; it gave all satisfaction which one may find in intellectual plesures when delicacy and elevation are absent. His mind was distinguished, but withdrawn and embarrassed for his soul was neither high nor profound. He was enlightened, subtle, flexible; as he was only open to that which was useful, he was full of profound disdain for the truth, and he did so little believe in virtue that his sight was darkened. Thus he did not see the beauty which truth and decency show, he did not even understand any more their usefulness which they so often have. He had a profound knowledge of human beings, but he knew them only through their vices. He was unbeliever in religious matters as the eighteenth century and sceptical in politics as the nineteenth; having no belief himself, he did not believe in the belief of others. He was, as it were, naturally fond of power and of dishonest, mediocre, facile, and plain courtiers to be really born for the throne. His ambition only, limited by prudence, never satisfied, nor did it ever carry him away; it always kept him near to the ground.

Louis Philippe and his queen were bourgeois in the extreme —no royal pomp and display for them. Unfortunately, the same fickle Parisians who had cheered for an end to all aristocracy were equally willing to jeer at the court of Louis Philippe, which they described as "ridiculous gatherings of tailors, drapers, and bootmakers." The new king's speaking style won as little respect as his court. One Paris wit described Louis Phi-

lippe's remarks before the Chamber of Deputies as "a sentimental jargon . . . a facile redundancy singularly incorrect:
Jean-Jacques with a touch of a kitchenmaid of the nineteenth
century."

One story which made the rounds in Paris society described
Louis and Queen Victoria walking in the garden when . . .

> . . . with true French politeness, he offered her a peach. The Queen
> seemed rather embarrassed how to skin it, when Louis-Philippe took
> a large clasp-knife from his pocket. "When a man has been a poor
> devil like myself, obliged to live upon forty sous a day, he always
> carries a knife. I might have dispensed with it for the last few years;
> still, I do not wish to lose the habit—one does not know what may
> happen," he said.

The memory of his earlier poverty-stricken circumstances
during the days of the French Revolution was never far from
the new king. Even with a personal royal income of £750,000,
he was still capable of announcing to his chief minister, "I am
telling you that my children will be wanting for bread!" Poor
Louis Philippe: He had been called by Paris (and in those days
Paris made the political decisions for all of France) to be an
ideal monarch; he was only capable of being father of a large
family who looked upon the throne of France as a suitable
means of earning a living. And there were many times when
the price of that living seemed far too high for Louis. As he
grumbled to one of his relatives:

> The crown of France is too cold in winter, too warm in summer; the
> sceptre is too blunt as a weapon of defence or attack, it is too short
> as a stick to lean upon: a good felt hat and a strong umbrella are at
> all times more useful.

Thus there were times when Louis Philippe was too bourgeois for even the bourgeoisie.

Aftermath

The ascension of Louis Philippe to the throne had been widely propagandized throughout France as an amalgam of love for the monarchy and love for republican principles. Louis early realized that the bourgeoisie had no lost love for the monarchy; he came to realize as well that the bourgeoisie also was far more interested in its own economic position than in "liberty, fraternity, and equality." The Citizen King learned to hate the Marseillaise, serving as it did as the symbol for pretended republican enthusiasm. The Paris mobs always insisted that he join in the chorus whenever the old revolutionary hymn was sung in his presence. On occasion a mob of Parisians would sing the Marseillaise again and again beneath the windows of the king until the poor harassed man came out and joined them in sheer self-defense. Once when one of his ministers expressed concern at the frequency with which the king was called upon to sing the Marseillaise, he murmured in reply, "Do not worry yourself, Monsieur le Ministre; I am only moving my lips; I have ceased to pronounce the words for many a day."

It seems that both sides to the bargain of a bourgeois monarchy, i.e., citizens and king, came to view the whole transaction with disgust. If Louis Philippe only moved his lips when he sang the Marseillaise, the wits of Paris also had their innings making fun of his republican pretensions, especially his trait of invariably shaking hands with everyone he met. In the years of the July Monarchy, a play was actually staged in Paris which portrayed the king (in the play the character was named "King

of the Shopkeepers") giving the heir to the throne the following
advice on the proper method for governing France:

> Do not be misled by a parcel of theorists, who will tell you that the
> citizen-monarchy is based upon the sovereign will of the people, or
> upon the strict observance of the Charter; this is merely so much
> drivel from the political Rights or Lefts. In reality, it does not signify
> a jot whether France be free at home and feared and respected abroad,
> whether the throne he hedged round with republican institutions or
> supported by an hereditary peerage, whether the language of her
> statesmen be weighty and the deeds of her soldiers heroic. The citizen-
> monarchy and the art of governing consist of but one thing—the
> capacity of the principal ruler for shaking hands with any and every
> ragamuffin and out-of-elbows brute he meets.

Thereupon the "King of the Shopkeepers" shows his son
how to shake hands in every conceivable position—on foot, on
horseback, at a gallop, at a trot, leaning out of a carriage. Such
a lampoon may have been slightly unfair to Louis Philippe, but
it comes uncomfortably close to the mark in describing many
of the politicians who have been spawned by political life in a
democracy.

Whatever else may be said of Louis Philippe's reign, this
experiment in the republican monarchy, presided over by the
bourgeoisie, seemed to satisfy no one—not the republicans, not
the bourgeoisie, certainly not the monarch. The king came to
detest the bourgeoisie, thinking them second-rate intellectually
and resenting their alleged "admiration" of the "Citizen
King." He once remarked, "I am like the fool between two
stools, only I happen to be between the comfortably stuffed
easy-chair of the bourgeois drawing-room and the piece of
furniture seated on which Louis XIV is said to have received
the Dutch ambassadors." Louis Philippe had been isolated
from both the nobility and the bourgeoisie by this shift of

power to the middle class, thus giving France a government respected by no one, not even the king himself.

The result of this unsatisfactory experiment in bourgeois rule was a lapse of political interest and a totally colorless regime. As Tocqueville recalled the period:

> No sooner had the Revolution of 1830 become an accomplished fact, than there ensued a great lull in political passion, a sort of general subsidence, accompanied by a rapid increase in public wealth. The particular spirit of the middle class became the general spirit of the government; it ruled the latter's foreign policy as well as affairs at home: an active, industrious spirit, often dishonourable, generally orderly, occasionally reckless through vanity or egoism, but timid by temperament, moderate in all things except in its love of ease and comfort, and last but not least mediocre. It was a spirit which, mingled with that of the people or of the aristocracy, can do wonders; but which, by itself, will never produce more than a government short of both virtue and greatness. Master of everything in a manner that no aristocracy has ever been or may ever hope to be, the middle class, when called upon to assume the government, took it up as an industrial enterprise; it entrenched itself behind its power, and before long, in their egoism, each of its members thought much more of his private business than of public affairs; of his personal enjoyment than of the greatness of the nation.

Soon after the Revolution of 1830, for which Bastiat had entertained such high hopes, he was named justice of the peace for the canton of Mugron. He remained in this position and continued his quiet, undisturbed life of study throughout most of Louis Philippe's reign. Years later he would look back to the years after 1830 as an unfortunate and rudderless interlude during which France was sliding into a morass of socialism. But that course of events had not yet become clear to Bastiat or to France.

CHAPTER 3

Freedom of Exchange

You have left our village, and now you are in Paris, that seething whirlpool . . .

THE 1830'S MARKED A CONTINUATION OF BASTIAT'S PEACE-ful country life. His 1831 appointment as Mugron's Justice of the Peace did little to alter his day-to-day existence. Two years later he was elected to membership in the General Council of Landes. He accepted even that small additional responsibility with concern, fearing that this might alter the quiet pattern of his days. Bastiat seemed determined to live out his time as a scholarly gentleman-farmer in the south of France.

Meanwhile, France of the 1830's gave the superficial impression of prosperity and progress. Railroads were stretching across France, messages zoomed by semaphore from point to point at unheard-of speed for a pretelegraphic age. Louis Philippe's Chief Minister, Guizot, had urged the middle classes to enrich themselves, and the bourgeois Frenchmen were busily engaged in that task. But not all was as cheerful and harmonious as it appeared: during 1835, several attempts were made on the King's life. For the next decade, Louis Philippe was periodically threatened. The unrest mirrored by these attempts was aggravated by the government's repressive attitude toward the press. Louis Philippe wanted to stop the publication of articles which might incite insurrection or assassination. In practice, the royal edicts were often used to suppress all dissent. As the result, public opinion reflected in the popular press seemed almost totally complacent, but beneath the surface simmered widespread discontent.

Napoleon's nephew, Louis Napoleon, sought to capitalize on that discontent and crossed the Swiss border in 1836, entering Strasbourg and urging the city's inhabitants to rise in rebellion. Louis Philippe exported the would-be revolutionary to New York. Several years later, Louis Napoleon tried again to overthrow the French monarchy. This time he crossed the English Channel, bringing with him a tame eagle, presumably to remind the romantic French of his uncle's imperial eagles. Louis Philippe this time exiled the incurably ambitious revolutionary to a castle in Ham, a village in northern France. Though the exile was announced as a life sentence, within six years Louis Napoleon had again escaped to England where he bided his time and prepared for a third coup, that was ultimately to prove successful.

In the midst of so many trials, Louis Philippe leaned heavily on the bourgeoisie to maintain his position. Only the wealthier middle classes were allowed the vote; and to insure their support the monarchy granted them special privileges. The power of government was used freely to feather the nests of some citizens at the expense of others. The working classes, already excluded from the vote, grew restive in the face of this "unfair" division of government favors. Meanwhile, industrialism was having its impact on France. By 1840, one of every seven Frenchmen worked in the new manufacturing industries. Thus a growing proletariat comprised a new element in French society. In the regulated French economy, shortages of housing became the rule rather than the exception. These shortages, plus the exclusion of the working classes from the vote, formed a reservoir of discontent which was soon exploited by a number of theoreticians and would-be social philosophers who promised that true "equality" could be attained if only France would adopt their particular scheme. Worse still for the French people, most of these schemes were based upon a desire for greater and greater government planning and control.

Previously the upper middle class had blamed the nobility for France's problems—all France was to be prosperous once political power rested in solid bourgeois hands. However, when the upper middle classes achieved political power, they found themselves subject to the same criticism: "Louis Philippe and his bourgeois regime are responsible for all our problems; all France will be prosperous once political power rests safely in the hands of the lower middle classes and the workers." As this new battle cry developed, the peasants sat back, watched the entire farce, and said nothing. Perhaps the peasants were wondering when their turn would come. Perhaps they were only amazed that the lust for political power could infect one class after another in precisely the same way.

Bastiat and the Tariff

One of the chief ways in which the bourgeoisie used political power to their own advantage and France's detriment was the tariff. As a member of a merchant family, Bastiat was especially sensitive to this issue. Thus it was the tariff which first caused Bastiat to question the uses of political power. In 1829 he had begun a study on the tariff and its injustices, but the Revolution of 1830 delayed printing for so long that the manuscript was never published.

Bastiat needed look no further than Bayonne, the city of his own career as a merchant, to see the harm done by trade regulations, restrictions, and tariffs. A walk among the empty warehouses and along the silent docks was an education in itself. Tariffs in France had been raised repeatedly in the nineteenth century—always raised and never lowered to any real extent. For Bastiat, violations of the free trade principles of Say and Smith were the self-evident reason for the growing discontent of the French people.

In 1840 the gentleman-farmer-scholar of Mugron decided to visit Spain and Portugal in the hope of establishing an insurance company. Since Bastiat was not distinguished for his interest in business affairs, it may well be that the trip was undertaken at least partially for its own sake. Though he traveled during the summer, he came down with a persistent cold that plagued him until he finally cut short his stay. But while in Madrid and Lisbon, Bastiat saw other nations making the same mistakes he had seen in France. In the process he developed a keen ear for ridiculous pro-tariff arguments. Later he described his impressions of the legislatures of Spain and Portugal:

> Some years ago I was in Madrid where I attended a session of the Cortes. The subject under discussion was a treaty with Portugal for improving navigation on the Douro. One of the deputies rose and said: "If the Douro is canalized, shipping rates for cargoes traveling on it will be reduced. Portuguese grain will consequently sell at a lower price in the markets of Castile and will provide formidable competition for our *domestic industry.* I oppose the project, unless our cabinet ministers agree to raise the customs duty so as to redress the balance." The assembly found this argument unanswerable.

> Three months later I was in Lisbon. The same question was up for discussion in the Senate. A great hidalgo said: "Mr. President, the project is absurd. At great cost you have set guards along the banks of the Douro to prevent an invasion of Portugal by Castilian grain,

and at the same time you propose, again at great cost, to facilitate that
invasion. It is an inconsistency to which I cannot assent. Let us leave
the Douro to our children in just the same condition as our forefathers
left it to us."

Bastiat never ceased to marvel at the excuses men would
advance for destructive practices which limited trade. It appeared that men of Spain and Portugal were to be protected
at all costs from the harmful effects of inexpensive and plenti-
ful grain!

The French people also enjoyed similar "protection." The
importation of grain and some other agricultural products was
totally forbidden. Frenchmen were not allowed to import tea,
since, in the language of a contemporary textbook, "this bever-
age affects the national character in giving the stern outlook of
those men of the north, while wine denotes a soft gaiety."
English iron and cloth were available at such low prices in the
French market that, for the "protection" of the Frenchman,
the July Monarchy was forced to institute steps which first
doubled the French price of English iron and cloth and finally
forbade any further importation.

While the rural population of France thus found its standard
of living somewhat lower as the result of "protectionism," the
living conditions in French cities were driven to unbelievably
low levels. "Protected" prices were maintained at a level far too
high for the wages of the time. In many cases, work was not
available at any price. Of 150,000 residents of Lyon, 100,000
were described as indigent. By 1840 there were 130,000 aban-
doned children in the streets of French cities. It seemed clear
to Bastiat that Frenchmen needed protection primarily from
"protection." Government interference in freedom of transactions was stifling the French economy.

Bastiat had ventured to publish some of his thoughts on the tariff, primarily as applied to the French wine industry. In 1834, 1841, and 1843, his pieces had appeared in print, but with little or no public attention or comment. As late as the mid-1840s, it seemed that Bastiat was to remain the gentleman-farmer with the dilettante's interest in public affairs. The turning point in his life came quite by chance.

At a time when anti-British feeling ran high in France, Bastiat's open-minded attitudes often made him the target for criticism among his friends when the subject of England arose. It arose one day with a vengeance in a Mugron discussion group to which Bastiat belonged. A French newspaper had quoted the British Prime Minister, speaking in opposition to a proposed measure, as saying that, if the measure in question were adopted, ". . . we will become, like France, a second-class nation." Bastiat's friends were incensed, and, as usual, turned to him as though he and "his British friends" were personally responsible for this insult.

Typically, Bastiat checked his facts before saying a word. He ordered back issues of *The Globe and Traveler* to check Prime Minister Peel's speech in an English version, discovering that the phrase, "like France" had been maliciously inserted in the French version by an Anglophobe translator. Bastiat won his argument; more important, he discovered the Anti-Corn-Law League and the free trade work of Richard Cobden. French newspapers had paid virtually no attention to the English free trade movement. The news that likeminded believers in freedom of transactions were engaged in a widespread campaign to bring free trade to a neighboring country brought a breath of excitement to Bastiat's life. From that day forward, Frederic Bastiat closely followed the work of Richard Cobden and the development of the free trade movement in England.

Cobden and the League

Richard Cobden was more French than English in his philosophic views. He drew his ideas from the eighteenth century and based his social thought on the assumption that human nature was perfectible. In this, Cobden was far closer to the French *philosophes* than Bastiat would ever be. Yet Bastiat would base his leadership of the French free trade movement almost entirely upon the ideas and organizational principles of his English mentor. Cobden had organized a splendid vehicle for the propagation of the free trade idea. Free trade speakers were on the hustings everywhere in England. Handbills and posters confronted Englishmen at every turn. Cobden and his most brilliant associate, John Bright, developed such a reputation for invincibility that soon parliamentary opponents of free trade were unwilling to appear against them on the debate platform. As Professor Dean Russell says, "It is almost certain that there was not even one literate person in all of Great Britain who had not read of the League and its work by the end of 1844."

Certainly Frederic Bastiat was deeply involved in the whole tariff question by the end of 1844. In the white heat of excitement generated by Cobden and his crusade, Bastiat produced by far his most notable writing to that date, a study of the influences of English and French tariffs on the future of the two countries. He submitted the piece to the prestigious *Journal des economistes,* painfully aware that several pieces he had written in the early 1840s had never found a publisher.

The editors examined this article by an unknown author from the provinces and realized that they had discovered a brilliant new economic thinker with a fresh analysis of the problems plaguing French society. The article was published in October 1844 and overnight Frederic Bastiat found himself an established author. Compliments poured into Mugron, together with requests for more articles. Bastiat immediately began contributing further to the *Journal* and also began gathering material for a history of Cobden's Anti-Corn-Law League. The correspondence with Cobden continued for the remainder of Bastiat's life.

From the time of the first article's publication in the *Journal des economistes,* Bastiat was launched upon a new career and a new phase of his life. The articles which he now began to pour out for publication in various journals would soon be published as *Economic Sophisms.* He was elected a corresponding member of the French Academy of Science. Mugron could not hold its gentleman-farmer much longer.

Bastiat had spent years qualifying to be called, and now the call had come. A genuine modesty and an unwillingness to leave his quiet, contemplative life caused him to delay for a time the enormous changes about to occur in his existence. He remained in Mugron to complete his book on Cobden and the English free trade movement.

At last Bastiat went to Paris in May 1845 to make publication arrangements for his book on Cobden. By July, he was on his way to England to meet the leaders of the free trade movement. He left Paris in triumph, with offers to direct the *Journal des economistes* and with suggestions that he should assume a university chair in political economy. The long years of reading and conversation with Coudroy now stood him in good stead. Paris found him a brilliant conversationalist as well as a fine writer. Bastiat was not a great orator, but with small groups of interested people, he was in his element. Perhaps his lifelong habits of study and concentration had convinced him that large audiences seldom retain anything of lasting value. At any rate, he generally seemed to act on the principle that "the best audience is an audience of one."

The same flair for direct and highly-individualized communication was also readily apparent in his writing. Returning to Mugron, he wrote easily and rapidly as twenty years of concentrated study and thought poured out of his mind and heart. *Economic Sophisms* had appeared in its first edition before the end of 1845; *Economic Harmonies* and many of his other essays also would soon find their way into print.

The Debate Begins

As Bastiat's frame spread and his arguments favoring free trade appeared in various newspapers and pamphlets throughout France, he immediately became the target for numerous public attacks. He was accused of pro-English sentiment because of his connections with Cobden and the League. This charge carried great weight in an age which found most Frenchmen actively hostile to anything English. Also, workers were told that Bastiat's ideas would lead to unemployment and starvation for the working classes. Every half-truth and nontruth imaginable was trotted out by the opponents of free trade.

Bastiat set a pattern which proponents of freedom could well follow in any age. He kept his temper and published refutations of the entire protectionist position, demolishing his opposition with simple language and easily-understood examples. Throughout, Bastiat reflected a sense of humor which illuminated the foibles of his age and which made the hard facts and tight logical analysis of his position far more popular and palatable than the usual grim preaching by reformers. Frederic Bastiat was perhaps the first of the happy libertarians, a special breed who are at once a delight to their friends and a thorn in the side of their enemies.

Writing in his Mugron study far from Paris, Bastiat returned to his central themes again and again: the myth of "overproduction"; emphasis upon the interests of the consumer (reminding his readers that we are *all* consumers); and special emphasis upon the idea that a fundamental harmony pervades the free market place. Bastiat thus popularized the idea of J. B. Say and Adam Smith that problems and distortions enter the economic scene as soon as government interference becomes the dominant force.

Building on Adam Smith, Bastiat stressed that free exchange permitted a division of labor,

> ... which makes it possible for each man, instead of struggling on his own behalf to overcome all the obstacles that stand in his way, to struggle against only *one,* not solely on his own account, but for the benefit of his fellow men, who in turn perform the same service for him.

Thus, specialization leads to increased production, of those items most desired by consumers, at a price which the consumers themselves are willing to pay. In free exchange, then, a natural harmony exists between production and consumption, between specialists and consumers of the specialty, provided only that the system is allowed to operate. The system, as Bastiat made clear again and again, can operate only so long as voluntary association and free choice prevail. The harmony of mutual interest is destroyed when the outside agency of the state introduces compulsion in place of voluntary cooperation. As Bastiat wrote:

> For a man, when he gets up in the morning, to be able to put on a suit of clothes, a piece of land has had to be enclosed, fertilized, drained, cultivated, planted with a certain kind of vegetation; flocks of sheep have had to feed on it; they have had to give their wool; this wool has had to be spun, woven, dyed, and converted into cloth; this cloth has had to be cut, sewn, and fashioned into a garment. And

this series of operations implies a host of others; for it presupposes the use of farming implements, of sheepfolds, of factories, of coal, of machines, of carriages, etc.

If society were not a very real association, anyone who wanted a suit of clothes would be reduced to working in isolation, that is, to performing himself the innumerable operations in this series, from the first blow of the pickaxe that initiates it right down to the last thrust of the needle that terminates it.

But thanks to that readiness to associate which is the distinctive characteristic of our species, these operations have been distributed among a multitude of workers, and they keep subdividing themselves more and more for the common good to the point where, as consumption increases, a single specialized operation can support a new industry. Then comes the distribution of the proceeds, according to the portion of value each one has contributed to the total work. If this is not association, I should like to know what is.

Do not this division of labor and these arrangements, decided upon in full liberty, serve the common good? Do we, then, need a socialist, under the pretext of planning, to come and despotically destroy our voluntary arrangements, put an end to the division of labor, substitute isolated efforts for co-operative efforts, and reverse the progress of civilization?

Paris

Though Bastiat's return to the peace and quiet of Mugron had given him an ideal opportunity to produce a steady flow of essays, he had been troubled by the feeling that still more needed to be done. There persisted in his thoughts the idea that a French free-trade movement patterned on Cobden's work in England was an absolute necessity before freedom of transactions could be brought to France.

However effective Bastiat had now proven himself as a writer and thinker, nothing in the quiet young man's life had shown the slightest flair for organization or for public life. But once again events were destined to redirect the life of Frederic Bastiat. A Bordeaux trade association had decided to petition the government for a Belgian-French customs union. Attracted by Bastiat's growing reputation as a foe of tariff barriers, the Bordeaux group asked his help in their campaign. Bastiat eagerly accepted. He wrote articles for the Bordeaux newspaper and made a series of speeches in which he soon turned the issue from the limited question of a customs union with one nation to the broader issue of free trade with all nations. By early 1846, the Bordeaux Association for Free Trade had become a reality.

Bastiat decided that the time had come for a nationwide free trade association. Fresh from his triumph in Bordeaux, he went to Paris to form an organization based on the Cobden model. The young author began to arrange a series of meetings, publish pamphlets and flyers, undertake speaking tours, and organize affiliate free trade associations in key French cities. He found his ambitious undertaking to be far more difficult than he had believed in his first enthusiasm. Writing to his old friend, Coudroy, Bastiat complained, "I am losing all my time, the association is progressing at a turtle's pace." Finding metropolitan Paris a tough nut to crack without wealth and position, he wrote his new friend, Richard Cobden:

> I suffer from my poverty; yes, instead of running from one to the other on foot, dirtied up to my back, in order to meet only one or two of them a day and obtain only evasive or weak responses, I would like to be able to unite them at my table in a rich salon, then the difficulties would be gone! Ah, it is neither the heart or the head that I lack, but I feel that this superb Babylon is not my place and that it is necessary that I hasten to return to my solitude.

It appeared that far more was involved in organizing a political movement than in being a successful pamphleteer. Bastiat now seemed ready to return to peaceful Mugron.

The lonely young man, writing what would later become the preface to *Economic Harmonies,* reflected on the choice involved in coming to Paris. Addressing himself in the second person, Bastiat wrestled with his hopes and his fears, leaving a moving portrait of a man torn between duty and desire:

My dear Frederic:

So you have done it: you have left our village. You have said good-bye to the countryside you loved so well, to your father's house within whose walls you enjoyed such complete independence, to your old books which still cannot get used to sleeping in neglect on their dusty shelves, to the garden where on our lengthy strolls we used to talk endlessly . . . You have bade farewell to that little plot of ground, the last resting place of so many dear ones with whom we associate our fondest hopes and our tenderest memories. Do you remember how the sight of their cherished graves renewed our faith and quickened our thoughts? But nothing could prevent your departure . . .

You could even bring yourself to leave the good farmers who looked to you not so much because you were their justice of the peace or because of your knowledge of the law, but rather for your native sense of fair play . . .

You could even leave your circle of close friends whose quick repartee, spilling over into two languages, and whose long-standing and intimate affection you held far more precious than fine manners . . .

You have turned a deaf ear upon your double bass—which seemed to have the power to stimulate your mind endlessly to new thoughts. My friendship could not deter you, nor even that complete freedom you enjoyed, the most precious of privileges, in regard to your activities, your hours, your studies. You have left our village, and now you are in Paris, that seething whirlpool . . .

I cannot believe that your head has been so turned by vanity that you would sacrifice your real happiness for a public acclaim which you know full well is not for you, and which in any case would be short-lived indeed. You would never aspire to being "in the papers of the

day the big man of the month." Such a course would be going counter
to all that you have stood for in the past . . .

It is, therefore, not due to the promptings of vanity that you have
turned your steps toward Paris. But what did induce you to go? Was
it a desire to do something for mankind? . . .

Like you I cherish all forms of freedom, and first among them that
freedom which is the most universally beneficial to all men, which
they enjoy every minute of the day and under all circumstances of
their lives—freedom of labor and freedom of exchange. I realize that
the right to posess the fruits of one's toil is the keystone of society and
even of human life. I realize that exchange is implicit in the idea of
property, and that restrictions on exchange shake the foundations of
our right to own anything. I approve of your devotion to the defense
of this freedom, whose triumph will usher in justice among all nations
and consequently will eliminate international hatreds and prejudices
and the wars that follow in their train.

The die had been cast; young Bastiat had decided that his most
important task now lay in Paris, on the firing line where the
issues were being debated.

One of the key figures in Bastiat's decision to stay on in Paris
was Michel Chevalier. A member of the Society of Economists
and influential in the publication of the *Journal des debats,*
Chevalier had been much impressed with Bastiat's writing and
had urged him to come to Paris. He was to become a close associate in the struggle to found a national free trade association.

During the spring of 1846, Bastiat and the group which
formed around him in Paris met to hammer out a Declaration
of Principles and to perfect their organizational plans. On May
4, Bastiat was named Director. The group had high hopes for
the new organization, believing that free trade was both an
important step toward securing other freedoms for the individual and a vital step toward ending war: "When goods don't
cross borders, armies will." From the beginning, the group

stressed that material benefits would come to the typical Frenchman as the result of free trade, but always insisted upon the broader moral point that peace and freedom were the really significant goals of the free trade movement.

The French government delayed for several months the issuance of formal authorization to the free-trade group, but Bastiat was coming to understand the workings of French politics more each day. He finally wrote a letter to a government minister, Duchatel, containing the correct balance of supplication and inside information. The letter provided the needed leverage, and the free-trade association was granted government approval for its activities, despite the resistance of the protectionist lobbyists who exercised so much influence in the French government of the 1840's.

The great significance of political leverage was becoming clear to Bastiat as he became more acquainted with Parisian society. He even thought for a time that he might enter national politics in 1846, even preparing a campaign brochure for the electors of his home district around Mugron. He was not nominated. Engrossed with his lectures, his writing and his attempts to organize the trade association, he was far too independent in his views and disinterested in the influence peddling that characterized French politics in the July Monarchy to undertake a serious political campaign.

Michel Chevalier was also unsuccessful in the 1846 elections, losing his bid for re-election in his home district. He and Bastiat returned to Paris where the Free Trade Association held an August dinner for Cobden. This dinner marked the climax of efforts to organize the group. With politics out of the way for the moment, the Association was about to launch a concerted campaign of public meetings and educational publications. The first public meeting of the Association was held August 28. Bringing together groups of legislators and key figures from the French world of affairs, Bastiat's group held several meetings during the fall of 1846. Public interest was keen, with turn-away crowds at each meeting numbering over 2,000. Soon LeHavre and Marseilles had followed the lead of Bordeaux and Paris in the formation of free trade associations. Meetings continued during 1847 and the early months of 1848. Bastiat and his friends had high hopes that they were on the road to as great a free trade triumph in France as Richard Cobden had achieved in England.

Le Libre-Exchange

Bastiat had concentrated from the beginning upon attracting favorable publicity to the issue of free trade. Aglow with success, he wrote Cobden, "Unquestionably, we are making progress. Six months ago, we didn't have even one newspaper for us. Today we have five in Paris, three in Bordeaux, two in Marseilles, one in LeHavre, and two in Bayonne." However, he came to realize as time passed that a newspaper devoted to free trade, published in Paris by the Association itself, would be a great asset. On November 29, 1846, his dream became a reality under his own editorship, when the first issue of *Le libre-echange* was published.

Many of the Bastiat's best pieces were to appear during the months ahead in the pages of this new journal. A full appreciation of Bastiat's satire can come only from reading all his work as he wrote it, but it is possible to catch the flavor of his wit with a sample or two. For example, his famous *Petition of the Candlemakers:*

From the Manufacturers of Candles, Tapers, Lanterns, Candlesticks, Street Lamps, Snuffers, and Extinguishers, and from the Producers of Tallow, Oil, Resin, Alcohol, and Generally of Everything Connected with Lighting.

To the Honorable Members of the Chamber of Deputies.

Gentlemen:

We are suffering from the ruinous competition of a foreign rival who apparently works under conditions so far superior to our own for the production of light that he is *flooding* the *domestic market* with it at an incredibly low price; for the moment he appears, our sales cease, all the consumers turn to him, and a branch of French industry whose ramifications are innumerable is all at once reduced to complete stagnation. This rival, which is none other than the sun, is waging war on us so mercilessly that we suspect he is being stirred up against us by perfidious Albion [England] (excellent diplomacy nowadays!), particularly because he has for that haughty island a respect that he does not show for us.

We ask you to be so good as to pass a law requiring the closing of all windows, dormers, skylights, inside and outside shutters, curtains, casements, bull's-eyes, deadlights, and blinds—in short, all openings, holes, chinks, and fissures through which the light of the sun is wont to enter houses, to the detriment of the fair industries with which, we are proud to say, we have endowed the country, a country that cannot, without betraying ingratitude, abandon us today to so unequal a combat.

Be good enough, honorable deputies, to take our request seriously, and do not reject it without at least hearing the reasons that we have to advance in its support.

First, if you shut off as much as possible all access to natural light, and thereby create a need for artificial light, what industry in France will not ultimately be encouraged?

If France consumes more tallow, there will have to be more cattle and sheep, and, consequently, we shall see an increase in cleared fields, meat, wool, leather, and especially manure, the basis of all agricultural wealth.

If France consumes more oil, we shall see an expansion in the cultivation of the poppy, the olive and rapeseed. These rich yet soil-exhausting plants will come at just the right time to enable us to put to profitable use the increased fertility that the breeding of cattle will impart to the land.

Our moors will be covered with resinous trees. Numerous swarms of bees will gather from our mountains the perfumed treasures that today waste their fragrance, like the flowers from which they emanate. Thus, there is not one branch of agriculture that would not undergo a great expansion.

The same holds true of shipping. Thousands of vessels will engage in whaling, and in a short time we shall have a fleet capable of upholding the honor of France and of gratifying the patriotic aspirations of the undersigned petitioners, chandlers, etc.

But what shall we say of the *specialties of Parisian manufacture?* Henceforth you will behold gilding, bronze, and crystal in candlesticks, in lamps, in chandeliers, in candelabra sparkling in spacious emporia compared with which those of today are but stalls.

There is no needy resin-collector on the heights of his sand dunes, no poor miner in the depths of his black pit, who will not receive higher wages and enjoy increased prosperity.

It needs but a little reflection, gentlemen, to be convinced that there is perhaps not one Frenchman, from the wealthy stockholder of the Anzin Company to the humblest vendor of matches, whose condition would not be improved by the success of our petition.

Commenting upon his own ridiculous example, Bastiat drove home the point:

When a product—coal, iron, wheat, or textiles—comes to us from abroad, and when we can acquire it for less labor than if we produced it ourselves, the difference is a *gratuitous gift* that is conferred upon us. The size of this gift is proportionate to the extent of this difference. It is a quarter, a half, or three-quarters of the value of the product if the foreigner asks of us only three-quarters, one-half, or one-quarter as high a price. It is as complete as it can be when the donor, like the sun in providing us with light, asks nothing from us. The question, and we pose it formally, is whether what you desire for France is the benefit of consumption free of charge or the alleged advantages of

onerous production. Make your choice, but be logical; for as long as
you ban, as you do, foreign coal, iron, wheat, and textiles, *in proportion* as their price approaches *zero,* how inconsistent it would be to
admit the light of the sun, whose price is zero all day long!

Frankly, is it not somewhat humiliating for the nineteenth century to
provide future ages with the spectacle of such childish behavior carried
on with such an air of imperturbable gravity? To be hoodwinked by
someone else is not very agreeable; but to use the vast apparatus of representative government to hoodwink ourselves, not just once, but twice
over—and that, too, in a little matter of arithmetic—is surely something to temper our pride in being the *century of enlightenment.*

Bastiat never tired of attacking the notion that France could
become rich by retarding production. In the *Courier français*
for September 18, 1846, shortly before *Le libre-échange* began
publication, he wrote:

> . . . there will be formed an association *in defense of labor with the left
> hand,* and the advocates of *left-hand labor* will have no trouble in
> demolishing all these generalities, speculations, assumptions, abstrac-
> tions, reveries, and utopian fantasies. They will need only to exhume
> the *Moniteur industriel* [a protectionist newspaper] of 1846; and they
> will find ready-made arguments against *freedom of trade* that will do
> quite as well against *freedom for the right hand* if they will merely
> substitute one expression for the other . . .
>
> *Work with your left hand, and not with your right.*
>
> The old system of *restriction* was based on the idea of creating obsta-
> cles in order to multiply job opportunities. The new system of *restric-
> tion* that we are proposing to take its place is based on exactly the
> same idea. Sire, to make laws in this fashion is not to innovate; it is
> to carry on in the traditional way.
>
> As for the efficacy of the measure, it is incontestable. It is difficult,
> much more difficult than people think, to do with the left hand what
> one is accustomed to doing with the right. You will be convinced of
> this, Sire, if you will deign to put our system to the test in performing
> some act that is familiar to you, such as, for instance, that of shuffling

cards. We can, therefore, flatter ourselves on opening to labor an unlimited number of job opportunities.

Once the workers in every branch of industry are restricted to the use of their left hands alone, imagine, Sire, the immense number of people that will be needed to meet the present demand for consumers' goods, assuming that it remains constant, as we always do when we compare different systems of production. So prodigious a demand for manual labor cannot fail to bring about a considerable rise in wages, and pauperism will disappear from the country as if by magic.

During the same period, Bastiat published a piece in the *Journal des économistes* entitled "Robbery by Subsidy." Accused of a high-brow attitude in previous debates, he responded:

People are finding my little book of *Sophisms* too theoretical, scientific, and metaphysical. Very well. Let us try the effect of a trivial, banal, and, if need be, a ruder style of writing. Convinced that the public has been *duped* into accepting the policy of protectionism, I have tried to prove it by an appeal to reason. But the public prefers to be shouted at. Therefore, let us vociferate:

Frankly, dear public, *you are being robbed.* This may be put crudely, but at least it is clear.

"Whoever by fraud has taken possession of a thing that does not belong to him is guilty of robbery." (Penal Code, art. 379.)

To rob: To appropriate by stealth or by force. (Dictionary of the Academie française.)

Robber: He who exacts more than his due. (*Ibid.*)

Now, does the monopolist who, by means of a law of his own making, makes it necessary for me to pay him twenty francs for what I could buy elsewhere for fifteen, take from me, by fraud, five francs that belong to me?

Does he not appropriate them by stealth or by force?

Does he not exact more than his due?

He does, indeed, it may be said, take; he does appropriate; he does exact; but not at all *by stealth* or *by force,* which are the characteristics of robbery.

When our tax accounts contain a charge of five francs for the subsidy that the monopolist takes, appropriates, or exacts, what could be more *stealthy,* since so few of us suspect it? And for those who are not dupes, what could be more *forced,* since at the first sign of refusal the bailiff's man is at our door?

Still, the monopolists need have no anxiety on that score. Robberies *by subsidy* or *by tariff,* though they violate equity quite as much as highway robbery does, do not violate the law; on the contrary, they are perpetrated by means of the law; this fact only makes them worse, but the *magistrates* have no quarrel with them.

These brief samples of Bastiat's irony should make it abundantly clear why his writing became so popular with the French people and so hated by the protectionists.

The French Free Trade Association

During the second year of the Association, Bastiat realized that the free trade movement was taking on an international flavor, with similar organizations springing up in Spain, Italy, Belgium, Sweden, and Germany. Bastiat found his work printed abroad in several languages and received invitations to speak across the European continent. A Prussian free trade leader promised a crowd of 10,000 people to celebrate Bastiat's arrival should he visit Germany.

The responsibilities involved in running the Association, plus his constant speaking and writing, took their toll. The already thin Bastiat became gaunt. But he would not slow his pace. There were times when the load seemed too great. He wrote his friend Coudroy, "My friend, I am not only the Association, I am the Association entirely. While I have zealous and devoted collaborators, they are interested only in speaking and writing. As for the organization and administration of this vast machine, I am alone."

Even in the face of these pressures, even when his own health seemed unequal to the task, Bastiat found time periodically to return to Mugron to visit his Aunt Justine who had raised him. The old lady, now alone and ill, remained one of the few people to whom this quiet and intense man gave an inkling of his inner feelings. To most of his associates, he remained a bit of a mystery. Capable of intense concentration and absolute clarity of thought, he was also capable of an almost unbelievable naivete. He frequently lost his way in Paris, and once, while presumably on his way to speak in Lyon, he arrived at an inn located some distance in the opposite direction.

The free trade movement in France was also going in the "opposite direction" by the end of 1847. Not even Bastiat's enormous efforts could disguise the fact that neither the government nor the people of France really understood the importance of freedom in transactions. The movement which had begun with such high hopes never attained the broad support necessary for its continued existence. The Association ceased to exist by the first months of 1848. Perhaps one reason for the rapid decline in the Association's fortunes was the difficulty in giving serious attention to the limited subject of free trade during the Revolution of 1848, a period when *all* social organization was being called into question. At least Bastiat had extended a measure of influence into the great political and social debate which lay ahead. The discussion of freedom was to provide an important antidote to the wild schemes of the social planners who emerged in 1848.

The Political Ramifications of Free Trade

Bastiat was the first to sense the vital nature of the *total* question posed by human freedom. At the height of the free trade movement, he wrote to Cobden, "Rather than the fact of free trade alone, I desire for my country the general philosophy of free trade. While free trade itself will bring more wealth to us, the acceptance of the general philosophy that underlies free trade will inspire all needed reforms." Sometimes his exclusive involvement in free trade issues chafed Bastiat. Addressing himself in the second person, he wrote:

> . . . why restrict yourself? Why hold your mind a prisoner? It seems to me that you have subjected it to a monk's regimen, with the unvarying crust of dry bread as your sole diet, for you are constantly gnawing away morning, noon, and night at a mere monetary question. As much as you, I long for commerce to be free. But is all human progress dependent upon this one freedom? In times past your heart quickened at the idea of freedom of thought and speech, still held prisoner by the censor and the laws against free assembly. Your burning desire was for parliamentary reform and for the thorough-going separation of the delegating and controlling powers from the executive powers in all these branches. All forms of freedom are interrelated. Together they all constitute a systematic and harmonious whole; there is not one of them that, when proved true, would not help to prove the truth of the others. But you are acting like a mechanic who is taking the utmost pains to explain an isolated piece of machinery down to its most minute detail, omitting nothing. One is tempted to cry out: "Show me the other pieces; make them move together; the action of one is explained by the action of all the others." . . .

For Frederic Bastiat, the problem of injustice, stemming from a lack of freedom, was the central fact of his analysis. What he called "the evil excesses of force" had become so "engrained in our ways and in our laws" that justice no longer seemed possible. Either men must be free, or society must be unjust. To Bastiat there was no middle ground.

In *Economic Sophisms,* he described the sad results of such injustice:

> I enter one of the cottages that cling to the French side of the Pyrenees.
>
> The head of the family receives only a slender wage for his work. His half-naked children shiver in the icy north wind; the fire is out, and there is nothing on the table. On the other side of the mountain there are wool, firewood, and corn; but these goods are forbidden to the family of the poor day-laborer, for the other side of the mountain is not in France. Foreign spruce will not gladden the cottage hearth; the shepherd's children will not know the taste of Biscayan maslin; and wool from Navarre will never warm their numbed limbs. All this is, we are told, in the interest of the general welfare. Very well. But then it must be admitted that in this instance the general welfare is in conflict with justice.
>
> To regulate consumers by law and limit them to the products of domestic industry is to encroach upon their freedom by forbidding them an action—exchange—that in itself is in no way contrary to morality; in short, it is to do them an *injustice.*
>
> And yet, we are told, this is necessary if production is to be maintained and the prosperity of the country is not to receive a fatal blow.
>
> The writers of the protectionist school thus reach the melancholy conclusion that there is a radical incompatibility between justice and the general welfare.

For Bastiat, of course, no incompatibility could exist between justice and the general welfare. All such arguments about such an illusory "general welfare" simply were so much moonshine put out by those who would replace freedom with force to further their own interests. Bastiat never tired of lashing out at "patriotic" arguments which called upon Frenchmen to give of their substance to support what he considered military adventurism. For example, in his little play centering upon two characters, James Goodfellow, the operator of a vineyard, and Blockhead, a tax collector:

BLOCKHEAD: You have laid in twenty tuns of wine?

JAMES GOODFELLOW: Yes, by dint of much toil and sweat.

B.: Be so kind as to give me six of the best.

J.G.: Six tuns out of twenty! Good heavens! You're trying to ruin me. And, if you please, what do you intend to do with them?

B.: The first will be given to the creditors of the state. When one has debts, the very least one can do is to pay the interest on them.

J.G.: And what has become of the principal?

B.: That would take too long to tell. A part of it was once invested in cartridges, which produced the most beautiful smoke in the world. Another part went to pay those who became crippled in foreign lands that they had laid waste. Then, when these expenditures of ours led to an invasion of our land by our good friends, the enemy, they were unwilling to leave without taking away some money, which we had to borrow.

J.G.: And what benefit do I derive from it today?

B.: The satisfaction of saying:

> How proud I am to be a Frenchman
> When I behold the triumphal column!

In Bastiat's attacks upon subsidies for some at the expense of everyone else, he was beginning to perceive that free trade was one tiny isolated corner of a much larger question: the necessity for freedom in all human activity. The young gentleman farmer had always been a man alone in the developing pattern of his life, but what truly set him apart from his times was his growing realization that government, *no matter who ran it, no matter in whose interests it was run,* could only be a harmful force let loose in human society whenever it exceeded its negative obligations to protect life and property.

Frederic Bastiat at 30 had believed that middle-class government could control and direct France. Frederic Bastiat at 45 had perceived that a government bent on managing human affairs could never bring justice and freedom to society, no matter who held the reins. Between 1830 and the mid-1840's, Bastiat had come of age while France had lost its way.

CHAPTER 4

Revolution: February 1848

We have tried so many things; when shall we try the simplest of all: freedom?

THE INDUSTRIAL DEVELOPMENT OF FRANCE OCCURRED under peculiarly trying circumstances during the 1840's. At best, an era of major transition brings with it dislocation of many sorts, but the Frenchmen of Bastiat's generation found themselves faced with more than an era of rapid change. They were also faced with a government determined to regulate and manipulate society. Those who were most sensitive to the current of affairs in France soon perceived that any truly independent business enterprise was likely to run disastrously afoul the French government and its complicated, contradictory legalisms. A far more promising road to success seemed to lie through politically-oriented business dealings. How much easier it seemed to run a business supported by a government tariff, a government monopoly, or even government capital.

If the productive businessman suffered under such a regime, the growing French proletariat suffered far more deeply. Real wages, what the paycheck of the French worker would actually buy at the grocery store, had been declining steadily since 1820. Prosperity seemed reserved for the few bourgeoisie who knew how to make government serve their purposes. There had been serious strikes during 1831–1832 and again in 1833, followed by the general strike of 1840. As the 1840s wore on, the picture grew even darker. Bad harvests in 1845 and 1846 had driven food prices ever higher. A severe industrial depression began in 1847, causing such widespread unemployment that over one-third of the population of Paris was on relief before the end of the year. At the very height of this distress, a cholera epidemic swept the city.

The French people would gladly have turned to anyone who offered relief in their time of distress, but they received only the shabbiest of platitudes and the most ridiculous analyses of their troubles. One member of the Chamber of Deputies received standing applause when he proposed that the depression of 1847 was due primarily to "external weakness" and "idle pacifism." It seemed that the troubles of France were due to an insufficiently militant foreign policy! While the Chamber of Deputies pondered the lost glories of French militarism, business after business failed throughout France. The number of businesses in Paris declined by over fifty percent during 1848.

The Corruption of French Society

The King's first minister during the crisis of the 1840s was Francois Guizot. He remained firmly convinced that France would prosper so long as only the wealthier members of the middle class had the right of suffrage. So long as the right people were running the government, surely the citizens of France need not worry. A few years earlier, Guizot had advised all Frenchmen to join the wealthy middle classes: *"Enrichissez vous, enrichissez vous."* Oddly enough, Guizot's private life was an absolute model of puritan rectitude, so out of character for the France of his time that even Louis Philippe had once remarked of his chief minister, "Guizot is so terribly respectable; I am afraid there is a mistake either about his nationality or his respectability, for they are badly matched."

However respectable Guizot was in his private life, he presided over an era in which prosperity was assumed to be found through courting the special privileges of government. The corruption implicit in such a system had spread throughout French society. As Priscilla Robertson, one historian of the period, has described it:

> The answer of the government to its growing unpopularity was corruption. If it could not placate the majority of the people because it did not trust them, it could at least control its own minority by bribes. Its candidates were returned to the Chamber by promises of bridges, railroads and hospitals to doubtful districts—a practice which led, incidentally, to an extraordinarily spotty development of railroad connections in those first years when they were being pushed through. Another common favor was the issuance of pardons or of exemptions from military service. Public morals sank below any recent remembrance. The director of the military bakery used state funds to speculate in wheat, leaving a tremendous deficit at his death. Two peers of France were actually tried and sentenced for dishonesty in a mining concession, and the case might never have come to trial if the principals had not quarreled and one published the other's incriminating letters. But the climax was the "affaire Petit," when Guizot himself, hitherto felt to be a rock of personal honesty, was shown to have paid 60,000 francs out of secret service money to recompense a man who had bought a place in the bureau of auditing and then not received the post.

Since the bourgeoisie had displayed such well publicized and self-congratulatory rectitude in their assurances to the people of France that middle-class control would be best for all, it is not surprising that the bourgeoisie, indeed, all men of property, became the hated scapegoats for Frenchmen in their hour of troubles. One cartoon of the times shows a dissipated loafer leaning against a lamp post and contemptuously eyeing a well-dressed bourgeois out for his Sunday stroll with his wife. The loafer is smoking a short, clay pipe, some of the fumes of which drift into the path of the bourgeois family and apparently offend their respectability. The bourgeois turns to the loafer, saying, "Begone!"

"It is time for you to be gone, you pig!" replies the Parisian man-of-the-streets. And there can be little doubt that it was an accurate expression of popular sentiment in 1848.

While hatreds mounted, the debates of the Chamber of Deputies seemed an exercise in futility. One of the deputies later wrote that:

> . . . these great orators were bored to death at listening to one another, and, what was worse, the whole country was bored with listening to them. France grew unconsciously accustomed to look upon the debates in the Chambers as exercises of the intellect rather than as serious discussions . . .

The government seemed blissfully unaware that not all was well in France. Corruption entered government dealings, and thence in turn corrupted all aspects of French life. Dishonesty became the order of the day for all classes. Complaints of false weights and adulteration made even minor transactions almost impossible. French wines were so often adulterated that they became difficult to sell abroad.

Perhaps those members of the Chamber of Deputies who blamed all of France's troubles on an insufficiently militant foreign policy were less stupid than they would appear at first glance. That analysis of France's afflictions may have been woefully inadequate; but their knowledge of French psychology was right on the mark. The French had always been a warlike people. A young journalist about to make a name for himself in the rapidly approaching revolution, Louis Blanc, expressed the sentiment of the typical Frenchman when he complained that France was a nation of warriors doomed to impotence because it was governed by the petty, shopkeeping bourgeoisie. The poor people of Paris were always jingoes. No matter how much Louis Philippe's innocuous foreign policy might have appealed to his fellow European monarchs, it left much to be desired in the hearts of French workers and students. The French poor suffered a miserable present, but they remembered the glorious days of the Empire, when all the world had waited with baited breath to see what the next move of Napoleon I would be. The lunatic fringe of Paris had made 17 assassination attempts on King Louis Philippe since 1830; and Richard Rush, American Minister to France, felt that the reason for these attempts at assassination had centered primarily on the fact that Louis Philippe had wanted peace for France.

Since Louis Philippe had been on the throne, France had acquiesced in treaties which involved the loss of Nice and Savoy to the south, plus an unfavorable change in the Rhine frontier to the east. The people of France hated the bourgeois July monarchy even more for France's lost glory than for France's hard times. Some of the nation's most wily demagogues were not above playing upon this fact of French politics for all it was worth. By 1848, discontent with the July monarchy had reached such feverish intensity that some radical change seemed unavoidable.

Bastiat on the Eve of Revolution

The last days of the July monarchy were also the exciting and busy days which saw Bastiat's development of the free-trade movement. He was publishing a weekly newspaper, speaking at meetings, corresponding with new free-trade associations which were forming in the provinces, writing letters and controversial articles in three different journals, and also doing some of the writing which would later prove his most lasting monument. He worked feverishly night and day. One of his French biographers describes Bastiat rising at dawn to scan the newspapers in search of a protectionist sophism, whereupon ". . . he would immediately seize his pen [and] demolish the sophism before breakfast. . . ." In the midst of all his other labors, Bastiat found time to visit Cobden, Bright, and the other key figures in the English free-trade movement. As rushed as Bastiat's own life was, he still found time to express amazement at the furious pace kept up by the Englishman, Richard Cobden. After visiting Cobden at his home in England one day shortly before Cobden left on a trip to Manchester, Bastiat remarked, "An Englishman's preparations consist of swallowing a beefsteak, and stuffing a couple of shirts into a carpetbag."

Such a hurried existence also characterized Bastiat's own activities. In addition to all of his other undertakings, he found time to deliver a series of lectures on political economy to a group of young Parisian students. Meanwhile, Bastiat struggled with a steadily weakening health. He had contracted tuberculosis, but was unwilling to slow the pace of his work long enough to take a much-needed rest.

The events of February 1848 put an end to Bastiat's teaching and an end to all hopes of further free-trade activity in France.

From that time on, events were to move so rapidly that Bastiat had to take quite another line of defense. On the eve of the February 1848 Revolution, Bastiat found himself living in a radically inflammatory and totally corrupt Paris. As the British author Thackeray described the city after his visit during those days, "Everything here seemed to me to be ranting, gaudy, and theatrical. Fictional liberty, fictional monarchy, fictional glory, fictional justice." Paris was in a state of ferment, a home for the ambitious, the malcontents, the political failures, the wild-eyed visionaries. By early 1848, Frederic Bastiat was sitting on a volcano about to erupt.

Prelude to Revolution

Since the wild days of 1789, Europe had looked to France as the home of revolutions. Based on performance, there was some justice in that reputation. It is also true that of the major European capitals, only Paris possessed a working class sufficiently organized to carry out an effective uprising.

Much of the working-class organization was due to the efforts of Louis Blanc, a bitter foe of the July monarchy. Blanc was willing to use force to achieve his ends, but was far from the most radical Frenchman in the Paris of 1848. Such men as Armand Barbès and Auguste Blanqui were far more bloodthirsty. They labored ceaselessly to build effective secret societies committed to "washing in the blood of kings." In 1839, both Barbès and Blanqui had been sentenced to death in the aftermath of an aborted coup. Under pressure from Victor Hugo, the always gentle Louis Philippe had commuted the sentences. Thus Barbès and Blanqui were ready to come out of prison and renew their agitation at the moment the monarchy tottered and fell.

The signal of the impending fall was clearly sounded in southern France on July 18, 1847. The town of Mâcon had arranged a banquet for its favorite son, the distinguished poet and historian, Alphonse de Lamartine. The banquet was spread outdoors and the banqueters found themselves drenched in a heavy summer thunder shower at the very moment when Lamartine was to begin speaking. But Lamartine's speech was such that no one of the 6,000 people attending the affair so much as stirred in his seat:

> It will fall, this royalty, be sure of that. It will fall, not in its blood like that of '89; but it will fall in its trap. And after having had the revolution of freedom and the counter-revolution of glory, you will have the revolution of public conscience and the revolution of contempt.

In Lamartine's phrase, "the revolution of contempt," the Revolution of 1848 is epitomized. The July monarchy fell less because it was overthrown than because no one was willing to support it any longer.

By the end of 1847, the custom of political banquets was well established throughout France. The mere act of buying a ticket for one of these banquets became symbolic of membership in "the Revolution of Contempt." The banquets became a vehicle for a more moderate expression of discontent, involving responsible politicians as well as radical revolutionaries. As one historian of the events of 1848 has described the banquet craze:

> Political banquets were an old English custom, and, faced with the prohibition against big public assemblies, the opposition members of the Chamber of Deputies adopted it in order to force the issue of reform upon the government. Lamartine, undecided as yet what party to help, was too cautious to attend more than one of these affairs— his own. The others were in the hands of liberal deputies, those who

wanted the English type of constitution, and the moderate republicans. The opposition that found its way into the Chamber under the existing election law was, as may be imagined, by no means the strongest anti-government force. But the Chamber was the place where infection could come to a head and burst, thus releasing other forces—the students, the secret societies, the disaffected national guard and the unpredictable people of Paris.

Soon the craze for political banquets forced the government of Louis Philippe to take stronger action. One of the largest and most popular of the banquets was scheduled for Paris in February 1848. Goaded by the abuses of the opposition, the government decided that the banquet must be banned. This was the signal for which Paris had been waiting. With cries of "Long live the Republic," the workers and the students poured into the streets, erecting barricades and waving the red flag. Fires were started all over the city. Soon troops were ordered to shoot arsonists on sight.

Fanaticism reached a fever pitch. Revolution and determination burned in the eyes of the Parisian people. One worker who anticipated the revolution walked about the streets carrying five loaves of bread beneath his arm, explaining, "For the three days; we always do such things in three days."

It was soon obvious that the people of Paris were considerably ahead of their leadership. The organizers of the political banquets now found themselves astride a tiger which was increasingly difficult to ride. Most of the political figures organizing the banquets had never intended the note of violence which was now everywhere in the air. Meanwhile, the leaderless people of Paris continued fanning their own revolutionary fervor. Lamartine could only stand by indecisively and wring his hands, believing that the people did not want Louis Blanc's socialism. Louis Blanc could only talk endlessly of how the people wanted more than Lamartine's republic. Neither Blanc nor Lamartine could believe that anyone might follow a really radical revolutionary like Blanqui.

If the opposition politicians no longer knew where France was going, some observers saw the future course of events with painful accuracy. One of these was the young Alexis de Tocqueville, then a member of the Chamber of Deputies. Addressing the Chamber on the 29th of January 1848, Tocqueville warned:

> Do you not see that they [the people] are gradually forming opinions and ideas which are destined not only to upset this or that law, ministry, or even form of government, but society itself, until it totters upon the foundations on which it rests to-day? Do you not listen to what they say to themselves each day? Do you not hear them repeating unceasingly that all that is above them is incapable and unworthy of governing them; that the distribution of goods prevalent until now throughout the world is unjust; that property rests on a foundation which is not an equitable one? And do you not realize that when such opinions take root, when they spread in an almost universal manner, when they sink deeply into the masses, they are bound to bring with them sooner or later . . . a most formidable revolution?
>
> This gentlemen, is my profound conviction: I believe that we are at this moment sleeping on a volcano. I am profoundly convinced of it. . . .

The Streets of Paris

Louis Philippe's First Minister, Guizot, became the focal point around which the storm center formed. The people on the barricades were calling for his immediate dismissal from the government. It is said that Louis Philippe had tears in his eyes as he embraced his Minister, but that he could hear the cries outside the Palace window which convinced him that Guizot must go. The Minister walked through the streets to the Chamber of Deputies, a rash and brave act in itself. With his face pale and his head held high, he personally announced that he had been dismissed from the government.

If Louis Philippe had really believed that concessions to the mob would appease the revolutionary fervor of the people, he was sadly mistaken. Immediately after Guizot's dismissal, affairs lapsed into worse disorder than before. Louis Philippe seemed unable to take decisive action. Delessert, Louis' Minister of Police, urged that action must be taken soon, but was unable to find anyone in authority willing to take the responsibility for giving the order to move against the political enemies of the Monarchy. Meanwhile, young revolutionaries were racing from barricade to barricade, insisting that the fall of Guizot was not enough and that the workers should march directly to the Chamber of Deputies and demand their full revolutionary rights.

The Chamber of Deputies

In the midst of the growing crisis, the Chamber of Deputies sat in a state of suspended animation. They seemed afraid to voice any mention of the dark forebodings which hung over the Chamber. Guizot's appearance before the Assembly to announce his dismissal as the First Minister of France interrupted a languid debate concerning a bill for the creation of a bank in Bordeaux. Guizot's dismissal at last forced the Deputies to face the issue. Alexis de Tocqueville painted a moving picture of that scene:

> The Opposition kept their seats, most of them uttering cries of victory and satisfied revenge; the leaders alone sat silent, busy in communing with themselves upon the use they would make of their triumph, and

careful not to insult a majority of which they might soon be called upon to make use. As to the majority, they seemed thunderstruck by this so unexpected blow, moved to and fro like a mass that sways from side to side, uncertain as to which side it shall fall on, and then descended noisily into the semi-circle. A few surrounded the ministers to ask them for explanations or to pay them their last respects, but the greater number clamoured against them with noisy and insulting shouts. "To throw up office, to abandon your political friends under such circumstances," they said, "is a piece of gross cowardice"; while others exclaimed that the members ought to proceed to the Tuileries in a body, and force the King to re-consider this fatal resolve.

This despair will arouse no astonishment when it is remembered that the greater number of these men felt themselves attacked not only in their political opinions, but in the most sensitive part of their private interest. The fall of the Government compromised the entire fortune of one, the daughter's dowry of another, the son's career of a third. It was by this that they were almost all held. Most of them had not only bettered themselves by means of their votes, but one may say that they had lived on them. They still lived on them, and hoped to continue to live on them; for, the Ministry having lasted eight years, they had accustomed themselves to think that it would last for ever; they had grown attached to it with the honest, peaceful feeling of affection which one entertains for one's fields. From my seat, I watched this swaying crowd; I saw surprise, anger, fear and avarice mingle their various expressions upon those bewildered countenances; and I drew an involuntary comparison between all these legislators and a pack of hounds which with their jaws half filled, see the quarry withdrawn from them.

Tocqueville went on to put his finger upon the reason for the 1848 Revolution, indeed, one of the prime reasons for the failure of many governments during the past 150 years:

I grant, however, that, so far as many of the Opposition were concerned, it only wanted that they should be put to a similar test in order to make the same display. If many of the Conservatives only defended the Ministry with a view to keeping their places and emoluments, I am bound to say that many of the Opposition seemed to me only to attack it in order to reap the plunder in their turn. The truth—the deplorable truth—is that a taste for holding office and a desire to live on the public money is not with us a disease restricted to either party, but the great, chronic ailment of the whole nation; the result of the democratic constitution of our society and of the excessive centralization of our Government; the secret malady which undermined all former governments, and which will undermine all governments to come.

As the Chamber of Deputies continued to waver indecisively, the people moved to take all power into their own hands. Bit by bit the Chamber began to fill with people from the streets of Paris. Many of them were armed. Soon the Deputies found themselves surrounded by revolutionary rabble who stood by eyeing the lawmakers of France. Their silence was more pregnant with meaning than the wildest of outcries.

If the Deputies were uneasy, they were probably no more uneasy than the revolutionary chieftains who were now called upon to take the next steps. Most of the revolutionary leadership had never intended that the entire affair should take such a violent turn, and they now found themselves ill prepared to assume any real leadership. While the Chamber of Deputies sat in the midst of the vast Parisian mob, the revolutionary leaders met at the Hotel de Ville in an effort to hammer out a provisional government. Lamartine was becoming the man of the hour by virtue of his impassioned oratory. Soon the dwarf, Louis Blanc, forced his way into the discussions of the "provisional government." He was borne aloft on the shoulders of workers. Thus a handful of men met in a small apartment in the Hotel de Ville, surrounded by complete pandemonium. The hotel was filled with the wounded from the early street fighting, still lying on their blood-soaked straw pallets. Every room was jammed with gesticulating students, workers, and intellectuals. In such an environment, the new government of France was taking shape.

Middle-Class Apathy

As larger and larger crowds milled aimlessly about the streets of Paris, all responsibility for policing the city fell upon the National Guard. The middle-class National Guardsmen were unwilling to face any serious possibility of putting down the Revolution. While it is true that most of the National Guard probably did not want a Republic, their failure to decisively support the Monarchy led inevitably to the fall of Louis Philippe. To compound the confusions of the National Guard, rumors spread through the streets that the government was massacring the poor people. Unable to take a decisive stand against the people, the National Guard drifted aimlessly, leaving Paris exposed to total disorder and the collapse of all authority. Meanwhile the middle class kept insisting to itself, amidst great quantities of hand-wringing, "It is the government's fault, let the government solve its own problems. Why should we get killed for people who have managed their business so badly." And yet in Tocqueville's sharp appraisal, ". . . this was that middle class which had been pampered for eighteen years: the current of public opinion had ended by dragging it along, and it was driving it against those who had flattered it until it had become corrupt." Louis Philippe must surely have pondered moodily upon the fickle and fleeting nature of human loyalties.

Soon the National Guardsmen were stacking their muskets

and fraternizing with the crowd. As one English observer in Paris at the time described the scene:

> . . . it would not have surprised us in the least to see a troup of ballet dancers advance into our midst and give us the entertainment de rigueur—the intermède. It was the only thing wanting to complete the picture, from which even the low comedy incident was not wanting. An old woebegone creature, evidently the worse for liquor, had fallen down while a patrol of regulars was passing. He was not a bit hurt; but there and then the rabble proposed to carry him to the Hotel de Ville, and to give him an apotheosis as a martyr to the cause. They had already fetched the stretcher, and were, notwithstanding his violent struggles, hoisting him on it, when prevented by the captain of the National Guards.

Soon all Paris was without public authority: not a soldier, not a policeman, certainly no National Guardsmen. The "people" filled the streets, gave the orders, and served as judge, jury, and executioner. In Tocqueville's words:

> It was an extraordinary and terrible thing to see in the sole hands of those who possessed nothing, all this immense town, so full of riches, or rather this great nation: for, thanks to centralization, he who reigns in Paris governs France.

Perhaps the best characterization of the great majority of Frenchmen during the Revolutionary excitement of February 1848 is that they were not overthrowing the government, but allowing it to fall. Louis Philippe put in a brave public appearance or two in the vicinity of the Tuileries, but it was obvious that he rallied no support from any segment of society. The crowds around the Tuileries grew so immense and impassioned that many had their lives crushed from them in the terrible suffocating mob. Within a few hours, a broken Louis Philippe slipped out of Paris, never to return.

Violence in the Streets

With the departure of Louis Philippe, the people seemed completely in charge at last. The Parisian students had been especially aggressive, conducting repeated marches to the Chamber of Deputies while singing the *Marseillaise* at the top of their voices. Not to be denied their part in the fun of revolution, the street urchins of Paris had indulged in their favorite sport of stone throwing, often pelting those in authority and the revolutionaries with an impartial enthusiasm. Casualties from the mounting violence numbered into the hundreds. One early clash between the people and the National Guard had resulted in 52 deaths from a single fusillade. Bastiat was in the streets throughout the night after the "massacre." He had immediately summoned two assistants and spent his time giving medical aid to the wounded, whatever their role in the Revolution.

The results of the "massacre" of 52 revolutionaries were not long in coming. Someone located a wagon on which all the corpses could be placed. A man stood on top of the pile, holding a torch aloft for the people of Paris to see the crime that had been committed. The torch lighted the body of a young woman on top of the pile of bodies with her bloody breast bared. All night long the funeral wagon went from place to place throughout Paris. The great crowd following the wagon went to the doors of home after home, waking people and forcing them out in the streets to view the bodies. Outside Paris, railways and bridges had been destroyed in all directions for a distance of some thirty miles. Little or no milk or food was allowed to pass into the city. The people in their wrath would allow no sign of disaffection. As frightened citizens cringed in their homes, crowds of ruffians, stepping over the dead bodies still lying in the streets, demanded that all houses acknowledge the advent of the new Republic by means of

colored devices or lamps placed in the windows. As one frightened observer noted, "Woe to the houses, inhabitants of which
remained deaf to their summons to that effect. In a very few
minutes every window was smashed to atoms, until at last a
timid hand was seen to arrange a few bottles with candles stuck
into them on the sill, and light them. Then they departed, to
impose their will elsewhere." Milk might not have been allowed in the city, but there was no shortage of wine. Many of
the men and women in the revolutionary mobs seemed un-
steady in their gait as they prowled the streets intimidating any
and all comers.

The same disgusted Englishman who watched the antics of
the Parisian population intimidating people in their homes,
commented on the entire revolutionary interlude with an absence of restraint not typically British:

> I have seen them during the seige of Paris, and I have no hesitation
> in saying that, for cold-blooded, apish, monkeyish, tigerish cruelty,
> there is nothing on the face of God's earth to match them, and that
> no concessions wrung from society on their behalf will ever make
> them anything else but the fiends in human shape they are.

As soon as Louis Philippe and his family had fled the Tuileries, the people burst in and, discovering the table set for lunch,
made great sport of playing great ladies and gentlemen. An
orgy of broken glass, destroyed furniture, and ravished art
treasures quickly followed. What could not be carried off or
smashed was burned. Those bent upon entering locked rooms
of the Tuileries found themselves too impatient to wait for the
location of a key and smashed in door after door with a pen-
dulum they had ripped from a great clock.

Watching the destruction of a city which he was powerless

to prevent, Alexis de Tocqueville murmured, with admirable understatement, "Believe me, this time it is no longer a riot: It is a Revolution."

Aftermath

Writing to his friend Coudroy several days after the worst of the violence had passed, Bastiat sadly reported that the task of cleaning up the city would be enormous. He went on to speculate that the task of restoring the city, indeed restoring all France, might prove far more difficult than merely removing the wreckage of revolution. He speculated that the real cause of the February Revolution had been a failure of freedom in French society. He wrote, "Can we imagine citizens, otherwise completely free, moving to overthrow their government when its activity is limited to satisfying the most vital, the most keenly felt of all social wants, the need for justice?" Looking sadly about him at the wreckage of French society, Bastiat wondered, "We have tried so many things; when shall we try the simplest of all: freedom?" In sum, Bastiat's view of the February Revolution was that the society which fell deserved to fall. But he could not find himself lending agreement to the brutal destruction which the Revolution had demonstrated. It seemed to him that lack of freedom had caused the problem, but he saw no sign that the current temper of the French people was likely to produce any superior result.

Alexis de Tocqueville also tended to fear the results of the Revolution, however much he had disapproved of the previous regime. He described the causes of the catastrophe:

Add to this the democratic disease of envy, which was silently permeating it; the economical and political theories which were beginning to make their way and which strove to prove that human misery was the work of laws and not of Providence, and that poverty could be suppressed by changing the conditions of society; the contempt into which the governing class, and especially the men who led it, had fallen, a contempt so general and so profound that it paralysed the resistance even of those who were most interested in maintaining the power that was being overthrown; the centralization which reduced the whole revolutionary movement to the over-master of Paris and the seizing of the machinery of government; and lastly, the mobility of all this, institutions, ideas, men and customs, in a fluctuating state of society which had, in less than sixty years, undergone the shock of seven great revolutions, without numbering a multitude of smaller secondary upheavals.

Both Bastiat and Tocqueville warned that, although the failure of middle-class democracy had brought on a revolution allegedly motivated by lower-class democracy, the real failing, the rabid insistence that great political power could somehow benefit the lives of men, still remained to plague French society. In Bastiat's words:

> You call this the triumph of liberty, when it is its final defeat. I tell you that the people which you so artlessly admire has just succeeded in proving that it is unfit and unworthy to live a life of freedom. Show me what experience has taught it! Where are the new virtues it has gained, the old vices it has laid aside? No, I tell you, it is always the same, as impatient, as thoughtless, as contemptuous of law and order, as easily led and as cowardly in the presence of danger as its fathers were before it. Time has altered it in no way, and has left it as frivolous in serious matters as it used to be in trifles.

Suddenly middle-class democracy had been swept aside, but all of its shortcomings, all of the human foibles and corruptions, remained to plague France. The people had won a great "victory," but now lacked leaders to tell them what the victory had been. Poor old Louis Philippe was gone, and no new scapegoat seemed readily available on the horizon.

Events in Paris triggered similar uprisings throughout Europe. The university students of Germany, the peasants of Italy and Hungary, were moved to imitate the actions of the Parisian populace, with results which proved even less beneficial. Perhaps the best analysis of the February Revolution is also the simplest. Political interventions, combining the abuses of a past monarchy and a present democracy, had combined to undermine the prosperity and the morality of the French people, leaving them without principle and without leaders, rudderless in the midst of a revolutionary storm that had not yet seen a lasting end.

CHAPTER 5

The Triumph of
French Democracy

. . . you cannot legislate fraternity without legislating injustice.

THE 1840s IN FRANCE HAD SPAWNED A HOST OF ENEMIES
for the Bourgeois Monarchy. Many men had seen the approaching revolutionary possibilities in France and were carefully preparing for their own role in the government which they
felt would follow Louis Philippe. As is usually the case with
power-hungry politicians, they found it far easier to agree that
the old structure should be deposed than to agree what new
structure should be erected in its place.

The self-styled "provisional government" which had been
meeting at the Hotel de Ville soon demonstrated that its members could agree on little else than their common animosity to
Louis Philippe. One French wit, viewing the membership of the
provisional government and their constant posturings and ma-
neuvers against one another, commented that it was ". . . as if
Providence had deliberately thrown together all varieties of
human pride, in order to show how little this sentiment could
accomplish." Several of the members maintained spies to keep
tabs on their colleagues.

Under the leadership (if that be a suitable descriptive term)
of Lamartine and Blanc, the work of the provisional govern-

ment staggered forward. Blanc and Lamartine were at personal as well as political loggerheads from the beginning. Meanwhile, the entire situation was badly complicated by the continuing revolutionary unrest in the streets of Paris. It seemed that the members of the Parisian mob were quite willing to walk into meetings of the provisional government and announce their demands. The clear threat of further violence hung in the air. The streets of Paris were still barricaded and the socialists and communists were threatening to overthrow the provisional government in just the same way that the members of the provisional government had overthrown the monarchy. La-martine, one of the most popular French poets and renowned for his oratory, tried again and again to pacify the mob. Once, in desperation, he shouted to the mob gathered outside the Hotel de Ville, "What do you want?" One member of the crowd shouted back, "Your head!" That ended the discussion for Lamartine, who retired inside the Hotel to attend further deliberations of the provisional government. Such comments, uttered by a Parisian workman in the revolutionary atmos-phere of 1848, were not calculated to reassure even the most ambitious of politicians.

Though a regime was finally established under Lamartine, he and his fellow members in the government never recovered from the enormous surprise involved when they found them-selves in charge of the French state. Unable to agree with one another, all the republicans in the new government found themselves faced with the socialists and communists outside the government who demanded "an equal division of property" and whose pointed slogan, "Bread or Blood!" did little to reas-sure the new regime.

The central fact of the new regime was that no one, not even Lamartine nor Louis Blanc, ever emerged as a leader of any real significance. This left the new regime too exposed to the pressures of the Paris mob at a time when the socialist agitators, themselves unwilling and unable to assume real authority, were willing to keep the people agitated as a means of embarrassing the new government. It was during this period that a thousand plans of every conceivable description were put forth for the salvation of the French people. All these plans had in common the use of great centralized control to achieve social objectives. These plans appeared in the newspapers, on street corner placards and in the mouths of soap-box orators wherever a crowd would gather. All inequalities of fortune, education, property, or even sex were to be done away with. Poverty was to be specifically outlawed. Work was to become a thing of the past. It was in such an environment that the new government assumed power. Under increasing pressure to proclaim a republic, the provisional government finally acquiesced when the crowd broke into the meetings of the "leadership" and unfurled a huge banner on which, written in charcoal, appeared the slogan, "The Republic One and Indivisible is Declared." Concluding a hard night of drafting decrees and distributing portfolios, the weary members of the provisional government greeted the dawn with a breakfast of black bread and cheese, washed down with red wine drunk from a cracked sugar bowl which was passed from man to man around the room. Lamartine murmured, "A good beginning for economy in government." In such a manner did the Second French Republic come into existence.

The first nation to recognize the new French Republic was the United States of America. The American Minister in Paris, Richard Rush, took it upon himself to applaud publicly the triumph of democracy which he felt he had just witnessed. Soon other diplomatic recognitions were extended to the Sec-

ond French Republic. Even Frenchmen began to believe that
such an entity actually existed. Just as Frenchmen of the 1789
vintage had called one another "citizen," and revolutionary
Russians of a later date would call one another "comrade," the
1848'ers referred to one another as "laborer." "Trees of Liberty" were soon planted throughout Paris, and decorated with
a variety of flags and ribbons commemorating the new regime.
Along the Champs Elysees, young boys took shots at a clay
image of Louis Philippe. For those who hit the statue in the eye,
the prize was a miniature statue of liberty. Enthusiasm and
good feeling ran high among nearly all sections of the population. Rumors were circulating that under the new Republic a
"laborer" would be able to live for nothing, while no one would
ever need pay rent again. Some of the property owners who
refused to cooperate in this grand new scheme soon found their
buildings decorated with black flags and surrounded by straw
piles which appeared suspiciously convenient in case arson was
later decided upon.

The first problem of the new government centered upon a
socialist demand that the red flag should be used to replace the
French tri-color. Soon a mob had gathered at the Hotel de Ville
to demand that the provisional government adopt a new flag.
A hasty conference with the financial advisers of the new
regime made it clear that the red flag would ruin all hope of
international credit for the new government. That settled it for
Lamartine, who went out and faced the mob, whose muskets
were leveled at him while he spoke. The drama of the situation
caused the spell-binder to rise to even greater heights than
usual, and he managed to produce a powerful surge of patriotism in the crowd, reminding them that the tri-color had gone
round the world in triumph. Thus passed the first days of
government by mob.

Priscilla Robertson's *Revolutions of 1848* contains a fascinating sketch of the man called upon to lead the new "government by mob":

> Lamartine was born an aristocrat, with more ties to the Bourbon than to the Orleans dynasty. In 1830 he seemed too conservative for the new government of Louis Philippe, and people expected that he would retire and write more of the lyrics that made him one of France's leading poets. But Lamartine wanted to be a statesman, and in 1833 won election to the Chamber. When people asked him whether he would sit on the right or the left, he laughingly answered "on the ceiling," for his design was to keep away from party intrigues for a period, well out of trouble, while he polished up his public speaking. In order to learn how to make his words purple and golden (as Louis Blanc assures us they were in 1848) he practised on social and humanitarian subjects rather than on political ones. It is no wonder that his colleagues did not know what to make of him, or that when he formally entered the left in 1843 its members were alarmed.

To Tocqueville, the head of the Second French Republic was an absolutely unprincipled politician:

> I do not know that I have ever . . . met a mind so void of any thought of the public welfare as his . . . Neither have I ever known a mind less sincere . . . When speaking or writing he spoke the truth or lied, without caring which he did, occupied only with the effect he wished to produce at the moment. . . .

The common rumor of the time was that Lamartine had pledged his support to the government of Louis Philippe in last-minute secret sessions when it appeared that the government might remain standing but had changed sides and immediately came out in favor of outright revolution, because the prospect of becoming President of the new Republic seemed the only means of staving off his creditors. Thus, many Frenchmen of 1848 believed that this unprincipled and ambitious head of the new regime had clutched at it as a last desperate effort to avoid his enormous debts. Surely the new Republic was launched in an inauspicious fashion.

Lamartine had already been a major political figure and a member of the Chamber of Deputies before the February Revolution. He and Bastiat had been in correspondence for some three years before the Revolution. Lamartine had publicly advanced the thesis that government had an obligation to supply jobs to all those able and willing to work. Bastiat had immediately challenged that assumption and Lamartine had written to him privately, admitting the truth of Bastiat's analysis. Lamartine professed himself to be so impressed with Bastiat's ideas that he spoke from the same platform as Bastiat during an 1846 meeting in Marseilles, endorsing free trade, the principles of freedom in general, and the work of Frederic Bastiat in particular.

The friendly association of the two men continued to the eve of the Revolution. In fact, Lamartine had written to Bastiat shortly before the outbreak of revolution, "If ever the storm carries me to Power, you will help me carry out our ideas." Bastiat was apparently offered a high position in the new regime, but preferred to retain his freedom of criticism.

And criticize he did. When Lamartine began to make speeches referring to the necessity for fraternity as enforced by government in various social welfare measures, Bastiat immediately rose to the occasion:

I happened to discuss this question with the eminent gentleman whom the Revolution lifted to such great heights. I said to him: "Only justice can be demanded from the law, which acts by means of coercion."

> He thought that people can, in addition, expect fraternity from the law. Last August he wrote me: "If ever, in a time of crisis, I find myself placed at the helm, your idea will be half of my creed."
>
> And I reply to him here: "The second half of your creed will stifle the first, for you cannot legislate fraternity without legislating injustice."
>
> When, under the pretext of fraternity, the legal code imposes mutual sacrifices on the citizens, human nature is not thereby abrogated. Everyone will then direct his efforts toward contributing little to, and taking much from, the common fund of sacrifices. Now, is it the most unfortunate who gain in this struggle? Certainly not, but rather the most influential and calculating.

Such frankness was not calculated to make Bastiat a favorite of the new regime.

The appointments of the new regime were no more attractive than the regime itself. The novelist George Sand was given a position writing propaganda in the Ministry of the Interior. A life-long socialist devotee and enthusiast for every left-wing cause, George Sand's first reaction was, "I have seen the people, grand, sublime, generous, the most admirable people in the universe." After a few months' experience in the regime, she wrote, "The majority of the French people are blind, credulous, ignorant, ungrateful, bad and stupid. . . ."

While the propagandizing was left to George Sand and her instabilities, the portfolio of finance was entrusted to a well-to-do Parisian banker. He took one look at the financial position of the new government and vowed that he would rather commit suicide than share responsibility for the government. Lamartine looked about for a replacement financier and discovered him in Louis Antoine Garnier-Pages, who promptly restored credit by the brilliant measure of declaring the notes of the Bank of France to be legal tender, *not redeemable in specie.* This in effect relieved the new regime of all its financial responsibilities, so long as it could force its worthless notes upon any of its creditors.

Labor arbitration for the new Republic was assigned to the Paris Chief of Police. Soon his office was running a free employment agency and had taken over the placement of all Parisian workers. The Chief of Police also greatly facilitated labor management relations by forbidding all strikes by police order. The new regime was nothing, if not enthusiastic! One of the especially effective means of handling the unemployed was to recruit them as members of the National Guard or of the *Gardes Mobiles.* Soon there were some 90,000 new members of the Guard in Paris. Neither the social role nor the coercive power of the state seemed to be shrinking under the new Republic.

Bastiat Comes to the Assembly

The radical turmoil of Paris under the new regime did much to alienate the French provinces. Elections for the new constituent assembly under the Second French Republic were pending, and the provinces were determined to curb the radicalism of the Lamartine regime by the election of a more moderate assembly. For years Paris had ruled France, neither wisely nor well, and the provinces were determined not to allow a socialist take-over. Alexis de Tocqueville described the situation:

> Meanwhile the general election was drawing near, and each day the aspect of the future became more sinister. All the news from Paris represented the capital as on the point of constantly falling into the hands of armed Socialists. It was doubted whether these latter would allow the electors to vote freely, or at least whether they would submit to the National Assembly. Already in every part of the country the officers of the National Guard were being made to swear that they

would march against the Assembly if a conflict arose between that body and the people. The provinces were becoming more and more alarmed, but were also strengthening themselves at the sight of the danger.

By this time Bastiat had determined that the events in Paris demanded that he make every effort to stand as a spokesman against the rampant socialism of his time. He returned to his district in Landes to campaign for the legislature. Soon he had founded a journal *"La république Francaise,"* in an effort to bring his ideas before the general public. Bastiat asked the question, "Now that we have torn down, must we not begin to build anew?" That "building anew" could only begin, he felt, when France truly had

". . . protection for all rights, those of the conscience as well as those of intelligence; those of property, like those of work; those of the family as those of the commune; those of the country as those of humanity. I have no other ideal than universal justice; no other banner than that of our flag: Liberty, Equality, Fraternity."

Bastiat met with success and was soon elected Deputy to the National Assembly. As the date approached for him to leave his beloved Mugron and return to the bitter debates and pressing problems which he knew would face him in Paris, Bastiat took stock of himself and his life. He had in his mind and in his heart the idea for one brilliant all-encompassing study which would serve as his statement of the proper social order. And he was desperately afraid that the life which he faced in Paris would prevent his completion of his idea. On the eve of his final election to the National Assembly, he wrote:

Here I am in my solitude. Would that I could bury myself here forever, and work out peacefully this Economic synthesis which I have in my head, and which will never leave it! For, unless there occur some sudden change in public opinion, I am about to be sent to Paris charged with the terrible mandate of a Representative of the People. If I had health and strength, I should accept this mission with enthusiasm. But what can my feeble voice, my sickly and nervous constitution, accomplish in the midst of revolutionary tempests? How much wiser it had been to devote my last days to working out in silence the great problem of the social destinies, for something tells me I should have arrived at a solution! Poor village, humble home of my father, I am about to bid you an eternal adieu; and I quit you with the presentiment that my name and my life, lost amidst storms, will not have even that modest utility for which you had prepared me!

His recurrent weakness, produced by tuberculosis and aggravated by Bastiat's refusal to take the long rest necessary for any effective cure, had now advanced to the point that he realized his mission in Paris might be a virtual sentence of death. He felt that he was leaving Mugron for the last time.

When Bastiat arrived in Paris, a great change had occurred in this provincial Frenchman since his first arrival in the city a few years before. In the earlier 1840s, Bastiat had entered Parisian society dressed in clothes of provincial fashion. As one of his biographers describes him, "He had not had time to call in the assistance of a Parisian hatter and tailor, and with his long hair, his tiny hat, his ample frock-coat, and his family umbrella, you would have been apt to mistake him for an honest peasant, who had come to town for the first time to see the wonders of the metropolis." The Bastiat of 1848 was far more cosmopolitan, arriving dressed in the styles of the time. More important, though his emaciated face and hollow voice betrayed the ravages of disease within him, there was some-

thing about the glitter of his dark eyes which made immediately clear to all his associates that Bastiat now possessed
both the worldly experience of Parisian society and a strong
sense of mission. Bastiat was determined to meet the tide of socialism head-on in the revolutionary Paris which he so distrusted.

Arriving from Mugron, Bastiat found in the capital 100,000
armed workmen, dying of hunger, but filled to the brim
with the wild theories and visionary hopes implanted in them
by demagogues. Another returning legislator described the
scene:

> I saw society cut into two; those who possessed nothing, united in a
> common greed; those who possessed something, united in a common
> terror. There were no bonds, no sympathy between these two great
> sections; everywhere the idea of an inevitable and immediate struggle
> seemed at hand. Already the bourgeois and the people . . . had come
> to blows, with varying fortunes, at Rouen, Limoges, Paris; not a
> day passed but the owners of property were attacked or menaced
> in either their capital or income: they were asked to employ labour
> without selling the produce; they were expected to remit the
> rents of their tenants when they themselves possessed no other means
> of living.

At last the National Assembly met on May 4, though it was
far from clear until the last moment whether the Assembly
would ever meet at all. It was expected that the Parisian population would immediately bring enormous and potentially violent pressures to bear to demand that the government remove
all guarantees of property, substituting guarantees of a livelihood for all Frenchmen and for the satisfaction of every
"need." Bastiat described the bill of goods which the Parisian
demagogues had sold to the people:

Poor people, what deception awaits you. . . . The whole mechanism
consists of taking ten from you in order to give you back eight,
without counting the actual freedom which will be succumbed in the
operation.

Bastiat had expected a difficult situation in the new Assembly, but the reality was even worse. Fifteen times during the first sitting of the Assembly, the members competed with one another in shouting, "Long live the Republic!" This was probably less from Republican enthusiasm than from a desire on the part of most of the individual members to demonstrate their alleged enthusiasm for egalitarian causes. An early decree of the provisional government had demanded that the representatives in the French Assembly should wear an extravagant revolutionary uniform, though few members actually did adopt that style of dress. The Assembly was a bedlam, filled with political hatred and jealousy and yet bound by fear of the Parisian mob.

In an attempt to imitate the National Convention which had convened following the Revolution of 1789, the men with the most radical and most revolutionary opinions immediately adopted the custom of sitting on the highest benches within the Chamber. Calling themselves the Montagnards, those on the highest benches were a mixture of old-school revolutionaries and new-school socialists, fearing and distrusting one another, yet united in their common left-wing cause. Tocqueville describes the self-styled head of the Montagnards, Caussidière:

I saw a very big and very heavy body, on which was placed a sugar-
loaf head, sunk deep between the two shoulders, with a wicked,
cunning eye, and an air of general good-nature spread over the rest
of his face. In short, he was a mass of shapeless matter, in which

worked a mind sufficiently subtle to know how to make the most of
his coarseness and ignorance.

Surely the few honest men who remained in the French Assembly—men of the caliber of a Tocqueville or a Bastiat—had their
work cut out for them.

The Struggle Begins

Lamartine was now at the height of his popularity. He had not
only been elected to the National Assembly by the city of Paris,
but had also been elected by eleven other departments throughout France! All parties looked to him as a savior. The socialists
regarded him as a man on the left. The anti-socialists regarded
him as the only possible leader who attracted wide enough
support to stop the socialist tide. This attitude of the anti-
socialists is very difficult to understand, considering the major
role which Lamartine had played in the February Revolution.
It can be explained only by the fact that the National Assembly
was so badly frightened by the revolutionary Paris with which
it found itself surrounded, was so blinded by its terror of the
people, that it temporarily forgot Lamartine's involvement in
the same revolutionary activities. Perhaps Lamartine looked so
much less frightening than the other revolutionary leaders that
the anti-socialists forgot to be frightened of him at all.

Whatever the reason for his power, Lamartine began to
make immediate use of it, generally for socialistic purposes of
which Bastiat heartily disapproved. While poor health prevented him from strong speaking performances, he neverthe-
less sometimes addressed the Assembly. On other occasions,
Bastiat wrote out speeches in a style in which they would have
been delivered and then published them in various pamphlets

and in Paris newspapers. As the result, Bastiat and his words were very much on the scene during the Lamartine regime, and were invariably in bitter opposition to the direction Lamartine was taking. Some of the lectures which Bastiat delivered to the socialists in these days must have taken great personal courage. They also reflected the intellect and principled position of a man who saw far more clearly than most the direction his country was taking.

Lamartine had proposed a national exposition, to be financed in Paris by government funds. He had pointed out how the expenditure of these government funds would be a tremendous boost to employment, painting a moving picture of all the painters, masons, decorators, costumers, architects, and other workmen who would thus find their position improved and who would then be able to provide necessities for themselves and for their children. Lamartine concluded his speech to the Assembly amidst cheers and approval, insisting: "It is to them that you give these 60,000 francs."

To the Assembly's cries of "Very good!", Bastiat replied, "Very bad!":

> Yes, it is, at least in part, to the workers in the theaters that the sixty thousand francs in question will go. A few scraps might well get lost on the way. If one scrutinized the matter closely, one might even discover that most of the pie will find its way elsewhere. The workers will be fortunate if there are a few crumbs left for them! But I should like to assume that the entire subsidy will go to the painters, decorators, costumers, hairdressers, etc. *That is what is seen.*
>
> But where does it come from? This is the *other side* of the coin, just as important to examine as its *face.* What is the source of these sixty thousand francs? And where *would they have gone* if a legislative vote had not first directed them to the rue de Rivoli and from there to the

rue de Grenelle [from the City Hall to the theatrical suppliers on the Left Bank]? *That is what is not seen.*

Surely, no one will dare maintain that the legislative vote has caused this sum to hatch out from the ballot box; that it is a pure addition to the national wealth; that, without this miraculous vote, these sixty thousand francs would have remained invisible and impalpable. It must be admitted that all that the majority can do is to decide that they will be taken from somewhere to be sent somewhere else, and that they will have one destination only by being deflected from another.

This being the case, it is clear that the taxpayer who will have been taxed one franc will no longer have this franc at his disposal. It is clear that he will be deprived of a satisfaction to the tune of one franc, and that the worker, whoever he is, who would have procured this satisfaction for him, will be deprived of wages in the same amount.

Let us not, then, yield to the childish illusion of believing that the vote of May 16 *adds* anything whatever to national well-being and employment. It reallocates possessions, it reallocates wages, and that is all. . . .

When it is a question of taxes, gentlemen, prove their usefulness by reason with some foundation, but not with that lamentable assertion: "Public spending keeps the working class alive." It makes the mistake of covering up a fact that it is essential to know: namely, that *public spending* is *always* a substitute for *private spending* and that consequently it may well support one worker in place of another but adds nothing to the lot of the working class taken as a whole. Your argument is fashionable, but it is quite absurd, for the reasoning is not correct.

Bastiat returned to the attack again and again as various socialist measures were debated before the Assembly. Socialist orators proposed universal credit, underwritten by government funds. They proposed the development of the Algerian colony, including large-scale subsidies for the colony, and even the relocation of a substantial number of Frenchmen. In item after item, ranging from government aid to the needy to the most elaborate plans for government control of the economy, the socialists, spurred on by pressures from the Parisian population, brought up measures which Bastiat analyzed and attacked. As he wrote at the time:

> Four orators are all trying to be heard in the Assembly. At first they speak all at once, then one after the other. What have they said? Very beautiful things, surely, about the power and grandeur of France, the necessity of sowing in order to reap . . .

> The modern socialist factions ceaselessly oppose free association in present-day society. They do not realize that a free society is a true association much superior to any of those that they concoct out of their fertile imaginations.

> The socialists who have invented these follies, and who in days of distress plant them in the minds of the masses, generously confer on themselves the title of "forward-looking" men, and there is a real danger that usage, that tyrant of language, will ratify both the word and the judgment it implies. "Forward-looking" assumes that these gentlemen can see ahead much further than ordinary people; that their only fault is to be too much in advance of their century; and that, if the time has not yet arrived when certain private services, allegedly parasitical, can be eliminated, the fault is with the public, which is far behind socialism. To *my* mind and knowledge, it is the contrary that is true, and I do not know to what barbaric century we should have to return to find on this point a level of understanding comparable to that of the socialists.

> The more one examines these "forward-looking" schools of thought, the more one is convinced that at bottom they rest on nothing but ignorance proclaiming itself infallible and demanding despotic power in the name of this infallibility.

National Workshops

Bastiat's constant exposure of left-wing failures and distortions did little to stem the socialist tide. The socialists were determined that the state provide employment for all Frenchmen. Under their influence, the National Workshops were established. Louis Blanc had long made this "right to employment" a major issue in French politics. Under his chairmanship, the Luxembourg Commission drew up a report advocating almost total state socialism. A series of communes were to be set up, supplemented by a full system of "social security." The National Workshops became one of the central features of the system as it was finally adopted by the Assembly. National Workshops members were given an insignia, a golden bee to wear on their caps. The officers wore woolen armbands. Soon the golden bees appeared everywhere in Paris, with the clear implication in the minds of many that the National Workshops marked the end of any truly private property in France. Frederic Bastiat warned that the National Assembly had before it an issue of the most vital importance:

> A new right clamors for entry into the Constitution: the *right to employment*. It does not merely ask for a place of its own; it lays claim wholly or partly to the place now held by the *right to property*.
>
> M. Louis Blanc has already provisionally proclaimed this new right, and we know with what success.
>
> M. Proudhon demands it in order to abolish property rights entirely . . .
>
> Thus, according to these political theorists, there is in property something unjust and false, a deadly germ. I propose to demonstrate that property is truth and justice itself, and that what it has within it is the principle of progress and life.

Most Frenchmen outside Paris hated the National Workshops and the man they felt primarily responsible for them,
Louis Blanc. They had also begun to distrust Lamartine because he seemed insufficiently strong to block the socialist tide.
Thus the hopes of property-conscious Frenchmen throughout the land centered on the newly elected Assembly. It
seemed that the people wished to take all power unto themselves; could the Assembly stop them? Soon the question of
force was clearly in the air, and the answer to how that question would be resolved lay with the largest force immediately
available, the National Guard. Since no one knew where the
loyalty of the National Guard would lie in a crisis, the Assembly, the Paris mobs, and the people of France watched expect-
antly.

Each day the crisis moved closer as the month of May 1848
advanced. More and more people spread aimlessly through the
streets. The galleries and even the floor of the Assembly were
always crowded with various members of the Paris population.
Each day as well, the National Workshops continued to grow.
By this time their population exceeded 100,000 workmen. The
question of the Workshops became so emotionally charged that
the question was never formally raised in the Assembly, for fear
of what the reaction would be in the streets of Paris. The
number of unemployed in the National Workshops then rose
to 120,000 and kept rising with no end in sight. The specter of
something for nothing was beginning to haunt France.

Throughout the month of May, even while the numbers in
the National Workshops grew larger and larger, various members of the Assembly were assuring the people of France that
all "unnecessary and unpopular" taxes would be removed. The
people of Paris were also asking for steadily larger government
grants for all sorts of projects—at the same moment when tax

reductions were being promised. At last Bastiat could stand no
more. He wrote:

> The public has been deluged, with an unlimited prodigality, by two
> sorts of promises. According to one, a vast number of charitable, but
> costly institutions are to be established at public expense. According
> to the other, all taxes are going to be reduced. Thus, on the one hand,
> nurseries, asylums, free primary and secondary schools, workships,
> and industrial retirement pensions are going to be multiplied. . . . The
> state is going to found credit institutions, lend to workers the tools of
> production, double the size of the army, reorganize the navy, etc., etc.,
> and, on the other hand, it will abolish the tax on salt, tolls, and all
> the most unpopular excises.

> Read the last Manifesto of the Montagnards which they issued in
> connection with the presidential election. It is rather long, but can be
> summed up in a few words: *The state should give a great deal to the
> citizens and take little from them.* It is always the same tactic, or, if
> you will, the same error. . . .

> Getting down to details, the signers of the manifesto say:

> *We demand the immediate abolition of taxes that fall on objects of
> primary necessity, such as salt, drinks, et cetera.*

> *Reform of the real estate tax, the octroi, and license fees.*

> *Justice free of charge, that is, the simplification of forms and the
> reduction of expenses.*

> Thus, real estate taxes, the octroi, license fees, taxes on stamps, salt,
> beverages, mail—all are to be done away with. These gentlemen have
> found the secret of keeping the *gentle hand* of the state energetic and
> active, while paralyzing its *rough hand.*

> Indeed! I ask the impartial reader, is this not childish and, what is
> more, dangerously childish? Why would people not make one revolu-
> tion after another, once they had made up their minds not to stop until
> this contradiction had been made a reality: "Give nothing to the state,
> and receive a great deal from it"?

Does anyone believe that if the Montagnards came to power, they would not themselves become the victims of the very means that they employed to seize it?

Undeceive yourselves. The demagogues would not know their business if they had not acquired the art of hiding the rough hand while showing the gentle hand.

Their reign will surely mean a jubilee for the taxpayer.

"It is on luxuries," they say, "not necessities, that taxes should be imposed."

Will it not be a happy day when, in order to load us with benefits, the public treasury is content to take from us just our superfluous funds?

Nor is this all. The Montagnards intend that "taxation should lose its oppressive character and should henceforth be no more than an act of fraternity."

Heavenly days! I am well aware of the fact that it is the vogue to get fraternity in everywhere, but I did not suspect that it could be put into the receipt of the tax collector.

The Approaching Clash

At the May 15th meeting of the Assembly, the Assemblymen suddenly realized that the streets outside the Chamber were more quiet than they had been since the new Chamber of Deputies had begun its meetings. The group of legislators realized that they were surrounded by something more than 20,000 men when the crowd at last revealed its approach with a single terrible shout. The stunned legislators kept their seats. The speaker who had held the floor continued his remarks. Another of the legislators came back from the door of the Chamber to push the speaker aside, announcing, " . . . General Courtais had ordered the *Gardes Mobiles* guarding the doors of the Assembly to sheathe their bayonets." Immediately afterward, people began to pour through every door, surrounding the Deputies with a mass of humanity. Some of the intruders were armed. Some were aggressive, others only astonished at having forced the legislature without resistance. All were in a state of feverish excitement. The day outside was sweltering, and the resultant temperature rising from the packed humanity soon made the chambers an unbearable place. Revolutionary slogans were muttered here and there throughout the great hall. One man pointed to a deputy, announcing to the group around him, "See that vulture down there? I should like to twist its neck." In silence and in fear, the Deputies still retained their seats. As Tocqueville recalls that horrible moment:

> It was then that I saw appear . . . in the tribune a man whom I have never seen since, but the recollection of whom has always filled me with horror and disgust. He had wan, emaciated cheeks, white lips, a sickly, wicked and repulsive expression, a dirty pallor, the appearance of a mouldy corpse; he wore no visible linen; an old black frock-coat tightly covered his lean, withered limbs; he seemed to have passed his life in a sewer and to have just left it. I was told it was Blanqui.

The revolutionary leader mounted to a commanding position where he addressed the Assembly, demanding that the Assembly should pay for the wrongs it had committed against the people.

All day long this extraordinary Assembly remained in session. The legislators waited for assistance to arrive, but there seemed to be no other living soul in the city of Paris. Tocqueville continues his narrative:

> This passive resistance irritated and incensed the people; it was like a cold, even surface upon which its fury glided without knowing what to catch hold of; it struggled and writhed in vain, without finding any

issue to its undertaking. A thousand diverse and contradictory cla-
mours filled the air: "Let us go away," cried some. . . . "The organization of labour. . . . A ministry of labour. . . . A tax on the rich. . . .
We want Louis Blanc!" cried others; they ended by fighting at the foot
of the tribune to decide who should mount it; five or six orators
occupied it at once, and often all spoke together. As always happens
in insurrections, the terrible was mingled with the ridiculous. The heat
was so stifling that many of the first intruders left the Chamber; they
were forthwith replaced by others who had been waiting at the doors
to come in. In this way I saw a fireman in uniform making his way
down the gangway that passed along my bench. "We can't make them
vote!" they shouted to him. "Wait, wait," he replied, "I'll see to it,
I'll give them a piece of my mind." Thereupon he pulled his helmet
over his eyes with a determined air, fastened the strap, squeezed
through the crowd, pushing aside all who stood in his way, and
mounted the tribune. He imagined he would be as much at his ease
there as upon a roof, but he could not find his words and stopped
short. The people cried, "Speak up, fireman!" but he did not speak a
word, and they ended by turning him out of the tribune. Just then a
number of men of the people caught Louis Blanc in their arms and
carried him in triumph round the Chamber. They held him by his
little legs above their heads; I saw him make vain efforts to extricate
himself: he twisted and turned on every side without succeeding in
escaping from their hands, talking all the while in a choking, strident
voice. He reminded me of a snake having its tail pinched. They put
him down at last on a bench beneath mine. I heard him cry. "My
friends, the right you have just won. . . ." but the remainder of his
words were lost in the din.

At last the leaderless crowd dispersed, and a new group
began to congregate around the Hotel de Ville, center for revolutionary activities in Paris. From that day forward, the legislators invariably carried a brace of pistols beneath their coats.
Another popular weapon for the men of the Assembly was a
ball of lead sewn into a short leather thong which was then
fastened to the arm, a sort of portable club. The streets of Paris
became as unsafe as at any moment during the earlier February

Revolution. Surely revolution was on the verge of erupting once again.

The incident which finally crystalized a total breakdown of order was the announcement that the National Workshops were to be disbanded. Costs had risen to such enormous heights that the Assembly could no longer guarantee payments. The leaderless mob now erupted into violence as the summer of 1848 began. France was in the throes of its second revolution within four months.

No one knew better than Frederic Bastiat the reasons for this uprising, though few were willing to listen at the time:

> . . . while the French people have been in advance of all other nations in the conquest of their rights, or rather of their political guarantees, they have nonetheless remained the most governed, regimented, administered, imposed upon, shackled, and exploited of all.

> France is also, and necessarily, the one nation in which revolutions are most likely to occur.

> And what remedy is proposed? To enlarge the domain of the law indefinitely, that is, the responsibility of the government.

> But if the government undertakes to raise and to regulate wages, and cannot do so; if it undertakes to assist all the unfortunate, and cannot do so; if it undertakes to assure pensions to all workers, and cannot do so; if it undertakes to provide workers with the tools of production, and cannot do so; if it undertakes to make interest-free credit available to all those clamoring for loans, and cannot do so; if, in words that we regret to note were written by M. de Lamartine, "the state assumes the task of enlightening, developing, increasing, spiritualizing, and sanctifying the soul of the people," and if it fails; is it not evident that after each disappointment (alas, only too probable!), there will be a no less inevitable revolution?

> Once we start from this idea, accepted by all our political theorists, and so energetically expressed by M. Louis Blanc in these words: "The motive force of society is the government"; once men consider

themselves as sentient, but passive, incapable of improving themselves morally or materially by their own intelligence and energy, and reduced to expecting everything from the law; in a word, when they admit that their relation to the state is that of a flock of sheep to the shepherd, it is clear that the responsibility of the government is immense. Good and evil, virtue and vice, equality and inequality, wealth and poverty, all proceed from it. It is entrusted with everything, it undertakes everything, it does everything; hence, it is responsible for everything. If we are happy, it has every right to claim our gratitude; but if we are wretched, it alone is to blame. . . .

Thus, there is not a single ill afflicting the nation for which the government has not voluntarily made itself responsible. Is it astonishing, then, that each little twinge should be a cause of revolution?

In the setting of another age in which social order is collapsing, we might well ponder Bastiat's question.

CHAPTER 6

Revolution: June 1848

Do what you will, gentlemen; you cannot *give* money to some without taking it away from others. If you absolutely insist on draining the taxpayer dry, well and good; but at least do not treat him like a fool. Do not tell him: "I am taking this money from you to repay you for what I have already taken from you."

TIME WAS RUNNING OUT FOR THE FRENCH GOVERNMENT BY the early summer of 1848. The National Workshops had become a total political, social, and economic monstrosity. The Assembly found itself faced with an enormous contingent of men, already organized in para-military fashion, who felt that the government owed them all they had been receiving and a good deal more. Any attempt to disband the National Workshops was likely to be greeted with revolutionary violence, yet every day that the Assembly delayed in that inevitable step, the monster grew more and more powerful and more and more rapacious.

At last the Assembly took the dreaded step, the National Workshops were abolished. But the corruptions of the dole had done their work well. The workmen refused to leave the city, and on the 22nd of June they marched through the streets in military formations, chanting endlessly, "We won't be sent away, we won't be sent away. . . ." The nonworkers then presented a series of arrogant demands to the Assembly, accompanied with thinly veiled threats of violence. On June 23rd, the troops of the National Workshops (and they *were* troops) began building barricades. The streets of Paris were to taste blood once again.

The first policy of Lamartine's government was to attack the barricades one by one, thus favoring a holding action rather than an all-out confrontation against the National Workshops people. The National Guard soon found that the task they had been assigned was difficult indeed. The situation seemed desperate. As one of the Assembly members describes the scene:

> On my return I met, in the Rue des Jeuneurs, a National Guard covered with blood and fragments of brain. He was very pale and was going home. I asked him what was happening; he told me that his battalion had just received the full force of a very murderous discharge of the musketry at the Porte Saint-Denis. One of his comrades, whose name he mentioned to me, had been killed by his side, and he was covered with the blood and brains of this unhappy man.
>
> I returned to the Assembly, astonished at not having met a single soldier in the whole distance which I had traversed. It was not till I came in front of the Palais-Bourbon that I at last perceived great columns of infantry, marching, followed by cannon.
>
> I found the Assembly very determined, but very ill at ease; and it must be confessed there was enough to make it so. It was easy to perceive through the multitude of contradictory reports that we had to do with the most universal, the best armed, and the most furious insurrection ever known in Paris. The national workshops and various revolutionary bands that had just been disbanded supplied it with leaders. It was extending every moment, and it was difficult to believe that it would not end by being victorious, when one remembered that all the great insurrections of the last sixty years had triumphed. To all these enemies we were only able to oppose the battalions of the *bourgeoisie,*

regiments which had been disarmed in February, and twenty thousand undisciplined lads of the Garde Mobile, who were all sons, brothers, or near relations of insurgents, and whose dispositions were doubtful.

But what alarmed us most was our leaders. The members of the Executive Commission filled us with profound distrust. On this subject I encountered, in the Assembly, the same feeling which I had observed among the National Guard. We doubted the good faith of some and the capacity of others. They were too numerous, besides, and too much divided to be able to act in complete harmony, and they were too much men of speech and the pen to be able to act to good purpose under such circumstances, even if they had agreed among themselves.

What saved the Assembly and saved France in its hour of crisis was the very desperation of the situation. Things were so totally out of hand, and the threat was so enormous, that the men of the French provinces realized that the revolt had to be put down at all costs. Thousands of men simultaneously rose up all over France and began the journey to Paris, entering the city from every conceivable direction. Men of every class, armed in every conceivable manner, these Frenchmen knew that their country could not stand another triumph of the Parisian mobs. Tocqueville summarized the result:

It was evident from that moment that we should end by gaining the day, for the insurgents received no reinforcements, whereas we had all France for reserves.

The struggle for the control of France had been bitter indeed. Many of the houses of Paris were left in smoking ruins. Debris filled the streets. Thousands had been killed or wounded. France was continuing its horrible object lesson for the world.

Bastiat Stands Against the Tide

Though it was true that the people of France had been deeply frightened by the June uprising, much as the Romans had been frightened by the barbarian invasions, it seemed that they had learned little enough in the process. Though there was a strong reaction against the lower classes and against the Parisian mobs, there seemed no clear understanding as to the real cause of the trouble. The French population had been sufficiently frightened to be bitterly opposed to revolution, but continued to favor the socialism and government interventionism which had produced the revolution. Revolution had been put down, but the tide of socialism was still running strong.

It was Frederic Bastiat's fate to be projected into the very path of that tide and to stand almost alone against it. The events of his entire life seemed a preparation for the impossible task which now faced him. It was in this difficult and thankless undertaking that Bastiat had his finest hour, as he struggled to bring to the people of France the understanding of their own problems and institutions which they so desperately needed.

Throughout his last great crusdade against socialism, Bastiat worked unceasingly, refusing to spare any attention for his rapidly failing health. Although he spoke before the Assembly only occasionally because he was having difficulty getting his breath, he turned out a flood of pamphlets and articles. In response to the socialist Louis Blanc, he wrote *Individualism and Fraternity*. In response to socialist arguments favoring abolition of private property, he had written *Property and Law*. As issue after issue arose in the Assembly or in the popular press, Bastiat dashed off an immediate and hard-hitting response. He also maintained a full-time round of duties in the Assembly itself, where he was an influential member of the

Committee of Finance. Writing to his old friend Coudroy and obviously envying his friend the peaceful repose of Mugron, Bastiat described his daily activities:

> I rise at six o'clock, dress, shave, breakfast, and read the newspapers; this occupies me till seven, or half-past seven. About nine, I am obliged to go out, for at ten commences the sitting of the Committee of Finance, of which I am a member. It continues till one, and then the public sitting begins, and continues till seven. I return to dinner, and it very rarely happens that there are not after-dinner meetings of Sub-Committees charged with special questions. The only hour at my disposal is from eight to nine in the morning, and it is at that hour that I receive visitors. . . . I am profoundly disgusted with this kind of life.

Though ill with tuberculois, Bastiat was undertaking a task beyond the powers of ten healthy men. Though he preferred the quiet and scholarly life, he was assuming the role of propagandist and popularizer, attempting to reach the people of France with the message of freedom at a time when the people of France demanded intervention.

From the beginning, Bastiat had spoken with such complete honesty and sincerity that even many of his enemies paid close attention to his comments and ideas. As one Paris newspaper, bitterly in opposition to Bastiat's position, phrased it:

> The doctrines of the writer-economist are not our own. But we must admit that he has posed this question with all the clarity of a practical man, and that he has offered, in support of his amendment, reasons of extreme gravity, which have made a profound impression in the Assembly. Mr. Bastiat is not a good public speaker; he hesitates, he gropes around, he searches for the correct expression and doesn't always find it. But if his thoughts liberate themselves laboriously, they finish by carrying the day, armed with conclusive arguments.

Bastiat never voted with blocs. Thus, he voted sometimes
with the Left and sometimes with the Right. In fact, the one
consistent feature of Bastiat's voting record was that he always
voted with the minority. In every sense, Bastiat was indeed the
man alone, standing against the tide of socialism and against
the corrupt and demagogic politics of his times. Principle was
proving a lonely pinnacle, but the man from Mugron pursued
his ideas with a deep concern for their truth, not their
popularity.

Bastiat demonstrated his principled stand from the first.
Even at the risk of antagonizing the strongly conservative vot-
ers in his home district, he took a stand against the conviction
of Louis Blanc when he was tried by the Assembly on charges
of conspiracy and insurrection. Louis Blanc was not only a
prominent socialist and author of the National Workshops
plan, but was also a personal foe of Bastiat. As Bastiat explained in a letter to his friend, Coudroy:

> Even though a person believes deeply in something, he must not
> assume that the opposite belief is necessarily evil. . . . Thus the only
> thing I could do was to examine the evidence itself to see if Mr. Blanc
> was really guilty of *the fact* of conspiracy and insurrection. I do not
> believe that he was, and no one who reads his defense of his actions
> can believe him guilty either.

In the prevailing climate of hatred and reaction, dominated by
a search for a scapegoat to take full blame for the discontents
of the French people, a man of Bastiat's principle was rare
indeed.

In Bastiat's one-man struggle against socialism, he was far
more concerned with the inept defenses of freedom put up by
his would-be colleagues than he was in any of the attacks

leveled against his position by the socialists. As he wrote in a troubled moment, " . . . the worst thing that can happen to a good cause is not to be skillfully attacked, but to be ineptly defended."

The Workers and the Demagogues

The ailing Bastiat reserved a special quality of invective for the demagogues who made such impossible promises to the workers of France:

> An atheist was railing against religion, against priests, and against God. "If you keep on like this," said one of his listeners, who was not very orthodox himself, "you are going to make a pious man of me."

> Similarly when I hear our callow scribblers, our novelists, our reformers, our perfumed, mincing pamphleteers, gorged with ices and champagne, stuffing their portfolios with gilt-edged securities, or getting richly paid for their tirades against the egoism and individualism of our age; when I hear them disclaiming against the harshness of our institutions and bewailing the lot of wage earners and proletarians; when I see them raising to the heavens eyes full of tears at the sight of the poverty of the toiling masses—a poverty with which they never have any contact except to paint lucrative pictures of it; I am tempted to tell them: "If you go on like this, you are going to make me indifferent to the fate of the workers."

> Oh, what affectation! It is the nauseating malady of our age! Workers, if a serious man, a sincere humanitarian, paints a true picture of your misery, and if his book makes any impression at all, a mob of reformers at once pounces on it. They turn it this way and that; they exploit it; they distort it; they exaggerate it; they carry its ideas to ridiculous or disgusting extremes.

> . . . Workers, yours is a strange situation! . . . Oh, if all you needed to console you was a clamorous appeal for philanthropy, for ineffectual charity, for degrading alms; if only big words—*organization, communism, phalanstery*—were enough, people would not stint themselves on your behalf. But *justice,* pure and simple *justice,* that

is something no one dreams of giving you. And yet would it not be *just* if, after a hard day's ill-paid work, you could exchange the little you had received for the greatest amount of satisfaction that you could obtain freely from any man on the face of the earth?

Bastiat went on to point out that the lust for political power which the demagogues engendered in the workers was the greatest possible disservice to them. Thus he described the dominant mood of France, "Hurrah for charity! Long live humanitarianism! Tomorrow we shall take the City Hall by storm."

The increasingly stooped, thin figure of Bastiat became a familiar sight in Paris, not only in the Assembly, but wherever men met to discuss the ideas of the time. Bastiat was tireless in striking down error wherever it appeared. He defended the classical economic position as set forth by Thomas Malthus, pointing out that the English economist had far more in mind than the constantly quoted passage in which he had discussed the arithmetic and geometric qualities of the food supply and the population. Bastiat understood that Malthus was entirely mistaken about the ultimate prospects for starvation of the human race, and yet had great merit as a proponent of classical economic principles. Once Bastiat publicly challenged Pierre Leroux, a French philosopher and editor of *Le Globe* after Leroux had written a chapter against Malthus. Bastiat began by quoting some of the opinions expressed in Malthus' *Essay on Population,* and realized, as he pursued the point, that Leroux did not actually know the work of Malthus. Never one to do things by halves, Bastiat asked, "You have refuted Malthus, but have you by any chance read him through from one end to the other?"

"I have not read him at all," Leroux replied. "His whole

system is set forth on one page and can be summed up in his famous arithmetical and geometrical rations. That's enough for me."

"Apparently," Bastiat said, "you care nothing for the public, for Malthus, for the truth, for conscience, or for yourself."

That night, Bastiat wrote:

> This is the way an opinion gains acceptance in France. Fifty ig-noramuses repeat in chorus some absurd libel that has been thought up by an even bigger ignoramus; and, if only it happens to coincide to some slight degree with prevailing attitudes and passions, it becomes a self-evident truth.

The inherent contradictions in the posturings of the Left were apparent to Bastiat. For example, he noted that the ex-treme Left was "the natural enemy of all imaginable govern-ments," yet at the same time advocated "absorption by the government of all rights and all functions." Bastiat was de-scribing the Left-wing radicals of all time when he commented, "The proverb is therefore false that says, 'Never the twain shall meet.' "

Another contradiction which Bastiat delighted in pointing out again and again was the fundamental fallacy in the assump-tion that government could do something for the people that the people would somehow not be expected to pay for to the last penny. Relief for the taxpayer was perpetually promised, yet seemed long delayed:

> A few days ago, people expected to see the mechanism of representa-tive government create an utterly novel product that its wheels had not yet succeeded in grinding out: *the relief of the taxpayer.*
>
> Everyone anxiously awaited the outcome; the experiment affected men's pocketbooks as much as it aroused their curiousity. No one,

then, doubted that the machine had sufficient impulsion, because when self-interest and novelty turn the wheels, it runs admirably at all times, in all places, during all seasons, and under all circumstances.

But as for reforms tending to simplify and equalize the costs of government and to render them less burdensome, no one yet knows what it can do.

People said: "You will soon see. Now is the time. This is a job for the *fourth session,* when public approval is worth something. [Bastiat here refers to the meetings of the Chambers held in every fourth year, prior to elections, describing a practice well developed in our own political life.] In 1842, we got the railroads; in 1846, we are to get a lowering of the salt tax and postal rates; we shall have to wait until 1850 for the reform of the tariff and a change in our system of indirect taxation. The fourth session is the jubilee year for the taxpayer."

Bastiat, of course, knew what most taxpayers still had to learn—government cannot devise means for giving back more than it has taken:

Do what you will, gentlemen; you cannot *give money* to some without taking it away from others. If you absolutely insist on draining the taxpayer dry, well and good; but at least do not treat him like a fool. Do not tell him: "I am taking this money from you to repay you for what I have already taken from you."

The Communist Threat

The new government made a great point of insisting that its policies were designed to stop communism. This appeal to the fears of the French people was fostered especially by one of the key ministers in the new government, Thiers. As Bastiat well knew, Thiers had been a powerful friend of government intervention, especially in the area of tariffs. Yet this same Thiers was now posing as a leader in the struggle against communism. As Bastiat caustically commented:

There is good reason to say that the ways of God are as infallible as they are inscrutable. For if you will just grant me for a moment . . . that protectionism, when it becomes widespread, becomes communism, just as a little carp becomes a big carp, provided that God lets it live, I shall show you how odd it is that a champion of protectionism should pose as the destroyer of communism; but what is still more extraordinary and still more reassuring is that a powerful organization that was formed to disseminate the theory and practice of communism (in so far as this is deemed profitable to its members) should today devote half of its resources to destroying the evil it has done with the other half.

This is, I repeat, a reassuring spectacle. It reassures us as to the inevitable triumph of truth, since it shows us the first authentic disseminations of subversive doctrines, frightened by their success, now concocting the antidote and the poison in the same laboratory.

As Bastiat pointed out in January 1849, the *Moniteur industriel,* a group designed to press for government intervention in favor of business, especially as regarded tariffs, was urging a similar extortion of other people's property that the same men were quick to decry when it was applied to their own property. He clearly described the strange self-delusion which blinds men from seeing the truth about themselves and their ideas:

What likelihood is there that the great manufacturers, respectable landowners, rich bankers, and able statesmen have made of themselves, without knowing or desiring it, the initiators and the apostles of communism in France? . . . There are many workers full of a sincere faith in the *right to employment,* and consequently communists without knowing or desiring it, who would not tolerate their being considered as such. The reason for this is that in all classes of society, self-interest influences the will; and the will, as Pascal says, is the principal organ of belief. Many industrialists, otherwise quite respectable, promote communism (under another name), as people always do, that is, on condition that only the goods of others are to be divided and shared. But as soon as the principle has gained ground, and it is now a matter of sharing their own property too, oh, then communism strikes them with horror. Previously, they circulated the *Moniteur industriel;* now they are distributing the book on property. To be astonished at this, one must be ignorant of the human heart, its inner springs, and its proclivity toward clever casuistry.

In a pamphlet entitled "Protectionism and Communism," Bastiat boldly and directly addressed the government's Minister, Thiers, demolishing point by point the entire argument for government tariffs or subsidies of any kind and demonstrating again and again that no difference in principle existed to separate the policies of government intervention from the policies of out-and-out communism. Both were engaged in a war on property.

The Proper Role of Government

In his continuing struggle against socialism, Bastiat warned that the present temper of the French people to expect government solution of all their problems would not only fail to solve the problems, but would generate a bureaucracy penalizing material prosperity as well as freedom. In one speech before the Assembly, he won the applause of his fellow Deputies with a statement against such bureaucracy:

I am a firm believer in the ideas of Malthus when it comes to bureaucrats. For their expansion in numbers and projects is fixed precisely by Malthus' principle that the size of the population is determined by the amount of available food. If we vote 800 million francs for government services, the bureaucrats will devour 800 million; if we give them two billion, they will immediately expand themselves and their projects up to the full amount.

Building on his insistence that all government intervention amounted to a war on property and therefore to communism, Bastiat attempted to contrast a proper social framework with the governmentally controlled framework of his time:

> We recognize the right of every man to perform services for himself or to serve others according to conditions arrived at through free bargaining. Communism denies this right, since it places all services in the hands of an arbitrary, central authority.
>
> Our doctrine is based on private property. Communism is based on systematic plunder, since it consists in handing over to one man, without compensation, the labor of another. If it distributed to each one according to his labor, it would, in fact, recognize private property and would no longer be communism.
>
> Our doctrine is based on liberty. In fact, private property and liberty, in our eyes are one and the same; for man is made the owner of his own services by his right and his ability to dispose of them as he sees fit. Communism destroys liberty, for it permits no one to dispose freely of his own labor.
>
> Our doctrine is founded on justice; communism, on injustice. This is the necessary conclusion from what we have just said.

In his most famous book, *The Law,* Bastiat described socialism and communism, under whatever labels they might appear, as a form of legalized plunder. Recognizing that the law is organized force, Bastiat made it clear that such legal plunder could only be *organized injustice.* He went on to emphasize that such organized injustice finally proves so corrupting to the fabric of society as to destroy all social progress and, ultimately, all individual development.

For the planner devoted to government intervention in the lives of men, such interference with personal development seems a small price to pay, since, "All of them look upon the relations between mankind and the legislator as the same as those which exist between the clay and the potter."

Disarmament

As a classical nineteenth-century liberal, Bastiat saw the close connection between tariffs and war. Thus, there developed in him the insistent impression that one of the primary means of maintaining great and steadily expanding power over the lives of its citizens was the capacity of the government to generate an atmosphere of crisis. One hundred years before conservatives and libertarians in America discovered what was being done to their society, Bastiat had already grasped the essence of what we would later call "perpetual war for perpetual peace." He therefore included French military adventures in the catalogue of government foibles which he attacked.

Insisting that there was a fundamental conflict between vast military expenditures and prosperity at home, Bastiat caustically dismissed the idea that government spending somehow produced prosperity. He insisted that money spent for some public purpose was at best only money which would have otherwise been spent for a private purpose, perhaps of more lasting value than cartridges, uniforms, military salaries, and troop ships. Speaking before the Assembly, Bastiat once suggested that the French army was totally out of proportion to the nation's needs. One member of the Assembly rose to his feet and shouted to Bastiat, "But in June [during the June revolution] you were not sorry to have the army!"

Bastiat responded, "You reproach me with the month of June. But I say that if we had not had such excessive armies, we would not have had the month of June." He then went on to suggest that, if there were indeed a national profit in increasing the size of the army, why would it not profit France to call the whole male population to the colors?

There is also some evidence that, during the late fall of 1849, Bastiat went to England as a secret but official delegate from the French government to discuss the possibility of arms reduction. Not much is known about that trip, but it is true that Bastiat and Cobden had earlier exchanged a considerable amount of correspondence on the possibilities involved. Surely Bastiat saw free trade and limited government as the ideal means for attaining lasting peace and genuine freedom. In his stand against military adventurism, he was, as in so many other things, standing on principle against the dominant emotional tide of his times.

Unpopular Causes

Frederic Bastiat's penchant for unpopular causes was perhaps most clearly demonstrated in his strong public stand against the proposal to outlaw industrial unions. The National Workshops plan and the resultant revolutionary disturbances had so aroused the French people that the Assembly was in the process of forcing through a bill rendering illegal any form of worker organization whatsoever.

On the day of the debate, the Assembly was so aroused that it was difficult for a speaker to make himself heard over the tumult. Weakened by disease and already entering the last year of his life, Bastiat rose to make this unpopular cause his own:

> Citizens, I do not bring into this discussion any partisan spirit or any class prejudice. I shall not seek to play upon your emotions, but the

Assembly sees that my lungs cannot struggle against parliamentary tumults; I need its kindest attention.

Speaking against Articles 413, 415, and 416 of the Penal Code, Bastiat warned that the Assembly was in the process of establishing a dangerous precedent when it outlawed peaceful organization of any kind:

> . . . gentlemen, an action that is innocent in itself is not criminal because it is multiplied by a certain number of men. When an action is bad in itself, I admit that if that action is performed by a certain number of individuals, one may say that it is aggravated; but when it is innocent in itself, it cannot become criminal because it is the deed of a great number of individuals.

Speaking over the constant uproar of the Assembly, Bastiat insisted that any law which prohibited strikes would be a law enforcing slavery under another name. He pressed the point that respect for the law could only be founded upon a legal system which repressed intimidation and violence. Once the law became an institution of intimidation and violence itself, all respect for law would be at an end:

> . . . only principles have the power to satisfy men's minds, to win their hearts, and to gain the consent of their consciences. They have asked us: "Do you wish to proclaim freedom simply out of platonic love of freedom?" I, for my part, reply, "Yes." Freedom may entail trials for nations, but it alone enlightens, teaches, and edifies them. Outside of freedom, there is only oppression, and friends of order should bear in mind that this is no longer the time, if there ever was one, when the union of classes, respect for the law, security of interests, and the tranquillity of nations can be founded on oppression.
>
> In France we love freedom very much, but we hardly understand it. Oh, let us try to understand it better! We shall not love it any the less.

The Sick Republic

What Bastiat struggled against was a very old democratic disease: a willingness to deny the rights of property to others and to substitute governmental authority for individual rights. While Bastiat stood on principle, most Frenchmen rallied around plunder. In so doing, in his willingness to stand as a man alone, he won the respect of his enemies. Even the old socialist, Proudhon could write, some months before Bastiat's death, "He is devoted, body and soul, to the Republic, to liberty, to equality, to progress; he has clearly proved that devotion many times with his vote in the Assembly. But in spite of that, we list Mr. Bastiat among the men who oppose us."

Always insisting that he vote in terms of principle rather than in terms of party or temporary popularity, Bastiat frequently left his constituents in a rather confused state. But his principles shone through the petty politics of the time, and the electors of Landes returned him to office for a second term.

As civilization fell apart around him, Bastiat continued to work with what strength was left him. He always returned joyfully to his retreat in Mugron, where he had an opportunity to recover from the tumult of Paris. But once his strength had returned in the slightest degree, he was back in the thick of the fight. Throughout this most difficult and demanding time he maintained an open and generous character, and remained optimistic about the future of the world. Across the top of a page of poetry which he especially liked, he wrote some advice to himself that we all might heed: "Don't calumniate civilization."

The more difficult and dangerous the times, and the more closely pressed men of principle might be, the more important it is to remember that generous and profound advice.

CHAPTER 7

Last Days

What gives me courage is . . . the thought that, perhaps, my life may not have been useless to mankind.

TIME WAS RUNNING OUT FOR THE SECOND FRENCH REPUB-lic and for Frederic Bastiat. Bastiat well knew that the end was in sight, not only for his mortal efforts, but for the sick republic which staggered on toward its rendezvous with the man on horseback. His name: Louis Napoleon.

Even as the committee met to draw up the constitution for the Second French Republic, the Republic was expiring. The Committee for the Constitution itself gave evidence of the sad state of affairs in France. Personally acquainted with the mem-bers of the committee whose duty it was to draft a new consti-tution for France, Tocqueville regarded some of them as "chimerical visionaries." One committee member, Victor Con-siderant, Tocqueville found especially discouraging for the fu-ture of the New Republic: " . . .[he] would have deserved to be sent to a lunatic asylum had he been sincere—but I fear he deserved more than that." Tocqueville described the other committee members as being totally unaware of any lasting principles or purposes, totally bewildered at the prospect of deciding the course of action for France:

All this bore very little resemblance to the men, so certain of their
objects and so well acquainted with the measures necessary to attain
them, who sixty years before, under Washington's presidency, so
successfully drew up the American Constitution.

When it was drawn up, the constitution proved almost unbelievably complex, guaranteeing a deadlock between President and Assembly, and almost insuring that a dictator would
step forward to break the impasse. The would-be dictator was
ready at hand. Louis Napoleon Bonaparte had twice attempted
inept coups and had been stopped each time with little more
than a pat on the head. He had been dismissed as an absurd
light-weight, quite incapable of harming France. Perhaps this
is why, in the balloting for the first President under the new
Constitution, so many of the French leaders threw their support to Louis Napoleon. Surely here was a man whom the
politicians could control. How mistaken they were.

None the less, all France soon sang the praises of Louis
Napoleon and fully three-quarters of the voting population cast
their support to him. 1848 and 1849 had been filled with violent
revolution, erupting first in France and then spreading to
Vienna, Munich, Milan, Berlin, and Rome. The times had
moved too fast and had been too frightening for many people.
Perhaps a milquetoast in the presidency would give time for the
tide of change to subside.

Bastiat had thrown his support to General Cavaignac as a
candidate in the presidential election. Even in the face of Louis
Napoleon's overwhelming popularity, Bastiat refused to give
ground. He told the electors of his District how he felt and
flatly announced that if they had other ideas and other hopes
for France than those which he expressed, then he was not the
man to represent them in office. The election of December 10,

1849, which swept Louis Napoleon into office made it clear that the people did indeed wish a change. Even then, Bastiat refused to compromise in any way. When the House of Deputies visited the new President as a group to offer their good wishes, he refused to accompany the delegation.

While the people of France wished to go in a new direction, they had no idea of *what* direction. The French have been notoriously quick to revolt against government which did not seem to do their bidding, but the same people have shown little capacity to chart their own course. This was evident in their desperate haste to write the new constitution, as well as their rush to Louis Napoleon as President. No working majority seemed to stand in favor of any principle. During the presidential election, there had been five different Napoleonic newspapers published in Paris, stressing a variety of positions ranging from the extreme Left to the extreme Right. Each claimed Napoleon's position as their own. Nothing could have displayed the confusion of the French people better than Napoleon's election after such a campaign. In Tocqueville's phrase, " . . . the world is a strange theatre. There are moments in it when the worst plays are those which succeed best. If Louis Napoleon had been a wise man, or a man of genius, he could never have become President of the Republic." In perspective, it becomes clear that the French were unable to achieve either lasting stability or a free society because they could not cope with their deeply inbred tradition of centralization. All power had been drawn into too few hands, and, while those hands constantly changed, the enormous centralization of power did not. As the result, the life of the Second French Republic was to be little longer than the time remaining to Frederic Bastiat.

At a time of such confusion and distress, the magic name of Napoleon brought with it a vision of prestige, glory, and order.

The French, of all European peoples, had been most addicted to martial glory and ready to accept any privation or disruption so long as it promised the extravagant satisfactions of a sweeping foreign policy. Louis Napoleon, with the unerring sense of the demagogic politician, perceived that a militant and breast-beating foreign policy, in the tradition of the first Napoleon, would provide the issue he needed to move far beyond the simple position of President of the Second French Republic.

Louis Napoleon is an interesting study of the ambitious politician. He hid his thoughts behind the grey-blue, almond-shaped eyes through which he calculated the world and its occupants. As one visitor described those striking eyes, "If they were the windows of his soul, their blinds were constantly down." He impressed one visitor to the Presidential Palace as "an obvious opium eater," because of the utter lack of personal effusion which he displayed. Because of his German background, he retained a lifelong difficulty with the French language, though his deliberate and calculated manner helped him to overcome the deficiency. Louis Napoleon's position as an alien to French culture is revealed in this anecdote by one of his close associates during his early years as political head of France:

> The struggle [to speak French without a German accent] lasted till the very end of his life, though, by dint of speaking very slowly, he overcame them to a marvellous extent. But the moment he became in any way excited, the f's and the t's and the p's were always trying to oust the v's, the d's and the b's from their newly-acquired positions, and often gained a momentary victory. There is an amusing story to that effect, in connection with Napoleon's first interview with Bismarck . . . The Emperor was complimenting the German statesman on his French.

"M. de Bismarck, I have never heard a German speak French as you do," said Napoleon.

"Will you allow me to return the compliment, sire?"

"Certainly."

"I have never heard a Frenchman speak French as you do."

However poorly Louis Napoleon spoke their language, he understood the French psychological need for martial glory, and promptly commenced a series of interventions in Roman, Polish, and Hungarian political affairs. Meanwhile, he gave the French people a steady diet of imperialistic and republican sentiment.

Having provided Frenchmen their entertainment, Napoleon-the-Little hastened to consolidate this political power. By the end of 1851 he struck. On December 1st, all the opposition members of the Legislative Assembly were arrested in their homes and rushed to prison cells. Napoleon filled Paris with his troops and the next morning announced that the Legislative Assembly was dissolved, that a new constitution had been promulgated which made the presidential term of office ten years instead of four. He then placed this before the people for ratification and the French rushed to embrace their man on horseback, overwhelmingly endorsing his new constitution. Less than a year later by almost unanimous vote, they crowned their president: Napoleon III, Emperor of the French. French politics had now come full circle.

Few Frenchmen were astute enough to recognize what had happened to them. Bastiat had realized all along that Louis Napoleon was a man who calculated to do France great harm. Alexis de Tocqueville had believed some of the Republican

mouthings of Napoleon and had accepted an appointment as
Minister of Foreign Affairs in the Second French Republic.
However, when the Republic ended and the Empire began,
Tocqueville realized his mistake and refused to take any further
part in what he regarded as a conspiracy against France. Unfortunately, the Tocquevilles and the Bastiats were in short
supply in the France of the 1850's.

Bastiat's Analysis of France in 1850

Even in the final laps of his race with death, Bastiat found time
to analyze the French political scene and accurately predicted
the end of republican government in France. During June of
1850, he retired to Mugron for a few days where he wrote the
most famous and compelling of his books, *The Law*. In this
work and in the other pamphlets and essays which he wrote
during the last months of his life, Bastiat described why no
society could hope to long endure under any political regime
which denied freedom to its citizens:

> No society can exist if respect for the law does not to some extent
> prevail; but the surest way to have the laws respected is to make them
> respectable. When law and morality are in contradiction, the citizen
> finds himself in the cruel dilemma of either losing his moral sense or
> of losing respect for the law . . .

> Unfortunately, the law is by no means confined to its proper role. It
> is not only in indifferent and debatable matters that it has exceeded
> its legitimate function. It has done worse; it has acted in a way
> contrary to its own end; it has destroyed its own object: it has been
> employed in abolishing the justice which it was supposed to maintain,
> in effacing that limit between rights which it was its mission to respect;
> it has put the collective force at the service of those who desire to
> exploit, without risk and without scruple, the person, liberty, or prop-
> erty of others; it has converted plunder into a right, in order to protect
> it, and legitimate defense into a crime, in order to punish it.

Bastiat analyzed the interventionist society point by point and found it wanting in justice on every hand:

Alas? I find here so many nascent abuses, so many exceptions, so many direct or indirect deviations, appearing on the horizon of the new social order, that I do not know where to begin.

We have, first of all, licenses of all kinds. No one can become a barrister, a physician, a teacher, a broker, a dealer in government bonds, a solicitor, an attorney, a pharmacist, a printer, a butcher, or a baker without encountering legal restrictions. Each one of these represents a *service* that is forbidden by law, and hence those to whom authorization is granted raise their prices to such a point that the mere possession of the license, without the service, often has great value. . . .

Next comes the attempt to set an artificial price, to receive a supplementary value, by levying tariffs, for the most part on necessities: wheat, meat, cloth, iron, tools, etc. This is . . . a forcible violation of the most sacred of all property rights, that to the fruits of one's labor and productive capacities. . . .

Next comes taxation. It has become a much sought-after means of livelihood. We know that the number of government jobs has been increasing steadily, and that the number of applicants is increasing still more rapidly than the number of jobs. Now, does any one of these applicants ever ask himself whether he will render to the public *services* equivalent to those which he expects to receive? Is this scourge about to come to an end? How can we believe it, when we see that public opinion itself wants to have everything done by that fictitious being, the *state,* which signifies *a collection of salaried bureaucrats?* After having judged all men without exception as capable of governing the country, we declare them incapable of governing themselves. Very soon there will be two or three of these bureaucrats around every Frenchman, one to prevent him from working too much, another to give him an education, a third to furnish him credit, a fourth to interfere with his business transactions, etc., etc. Where will we be led by the illusion that impels us to believe that the state is a person who has an inexhaustible fortune independent of ours? . . .

I believe that we are entering on a path in which plunder, under very gentle, very subtle, very ingenious forms, embellished with the beautiful names of solidarity and fraternity, is going to assume proportions the extent of which the imagination hardly dares to measure. Here is how it will be done: Under the name of the *state* the citizens taken collectively are considered as a real being, having its own life, its own wealth, independently of the lives and the wealth of the citizens themselves; and then each addresses this fictitious being, some to obtain from it education, others employment, others credit, others food, etc., etc. Now the state can give nothing to the citizens that it has not first taken from them. The only effects of its intermediation are . . . a great dispersion of forces . . . , for everyone will try to turn over as little as possible to the public treasury and to take as much as possible out of it. In other words, the public treasury will be pillaged. And do we not see something similar happening today? What class does not solicit the favors of the state? It would seem as if the principle of life resided in it. Aside from the innumerable horde of its own agents, agriculture, manufacturing, commerce, the arts, the theatre, the colonies, and the shipping industry expect everything from it. They want it to clear and irrigate land, to colonize, to teach, and even to amuse. Each begs a bounty, a subsidy, an incentive, and especially the *gratuitous* gift of certain services, such as education and credit. And why not ask the state for the gratuitous gift of all services? Why not require the state to provide all the citizens with food, drink, clothing, and shelter free of charge?

And what is the final result of thus viewing the law and the state in such a perverted light? Bastiat warned that the price was high, and that the perversion in political terms would finally be a perversion of all social institutions as well, finally destroying society itself:

The law is no longer the refuge of the oppressed, but the arm of the oppressor! The law is no longer a shield, but a sword! The law no longer holds a balance in its august hands, but false weights and false keys! And you want society to be well ordered!

Your principle has placed these words above the entrance of the legislative chamber: "Whosoever acquires any influence here can obtain his share of legal plunder."

And what has been the result? All classes have flung themselves upon the doors of the chamber, crying: "A share of the plunder for me, for me!" . . .

And are you not appalled by the immense, radical, and deplorable innovation which will be introduced into the world on the day when the law itself is authorized to commit the very crime that it is its function to punish—on the day when it is turned, in theory and in practice, against liberty and property?

You deplore the symptoms that modern society exhibits; you shudder at the disorder that prevails in institutions and ideas. But is it not your principle that has perverted everything, both ideas and institutions?

Thus Bastiat perceived the cycle. Undue government intervention in the lives of men inevitably produces legalized injustice, which leads to a lack of respect for the law, indeed for all authority and institutions. An immoral social order breeds immoral citizens. Soon the social fabric itself disintegrates. For societies as well as individuals, the wages of sin *is* death.

In failing health and in realization that the burden he had been carrying must pass to others, Bastiat left behind advice for those who would continue the struggle. He warned that political power was the cause of France's social decline and could never provide solutions to the problem. He asked that Frenchmen look outside the political arena and concluded:

. . . there is only one remedy: time. People have to learn, through hard experience, the enormous disadvantage there is in plundering one another. . . .

And this goes on until the people learn to recognize and defend their true interests. Thus, we always reach the same conclusion: The only remedy is in the progressive enlightenment of public opinion.

The Race with Death

When a man has spent his first forty-five years in solitude and quiet preparation, only a crisis which he regards as vitally important will cause him to leave that self-imposed isolation. For Frederic Bastiat, that crisis was the rampant socialism which so savagely attacked his native France. And the crisis was sufficiently pressing upon Bastiat that, once he had entered the fray, he drove himself unmercifully to devote all his energies to the task at hand. His last major work was to be *Economic Harmonies,* a sustained intellectual effort that literally consumed his life. The idea for *Economic Harmonies* had been growing on him for some years. In 1845, he had written Coudroy,

> If my little treatise of the *Economic Sophisms* is successful, we may follow it up by another entitled *Social Harmonies.* It would be of the greatest utility for it would meet the desires of an age in search of artificial harmonies and organizations, by demonstrating the beauty, order, and progressive principle of the natural and providential harmonies.

Two years later, in the midst of his pressing duties in Paris, he was still struggling to find time to write the work he envisioned, "Oh, that the Divine Goodness would give me yet another year of strength, and permit me to explain to my young fellow-citizens what I regard as the true social theory. . . . I should then without regret, with joy, resign my life into His hands!"

In April 1849 Bastiat wrote Coudroy that at last he was about ready to work out his theory in detail. He felt the ideas involved had been running through some of his articles for years, but that he needed the opportunity to sit down and produce his major work in a clearly organized and complete form. In another letter he told Coudroy that he must soon leave Paris because of his failing health. He hoped that his breathing might improve in the comparatively fresh air of the country, adding, "I must renounce public life, and all my ambition now is to have three or four months of tranquillity to write my poor *Economic Harmonies*. They are in my head, but I fear they will never leave it."

One great idea filled his mind:

> Men's interests, rightly understood, are harmonious with one another, and the inner light that reveals them to men shines with an ever more vivid brilliance. Hence, their individual and collective efforts, their experience, their gropings, even their disappointments, their competition—in a word, their freedom—make men gravitate toward that unity which is the expression of the laws of their nature and the consummation of the common good.

Working feverishly, Bastiat poured forth his ideas. One can sense in the concluding chapter of *Harmonies* the desperate entanglement of thoughts which he had not the time to clearly organize and express. *Harmonies* appeared early in 1850 and was treated coldly by the critics, even by many of Bastiat's former colleagues in the free trade movement. Undaunted, he began work on a second volume of the *Harmonies*, which he was destined never to complete. Increasingly aware that he might not live to consummate his work, he speculated on the possibility of letting his old friend Coudroy finish the book, but decided that he and he alone could do the job that he wanted done. Bastiat simply lacked time to finish the work to his own satisfaction. Yet, the quality of his writing was such that today

Harmonies stands as a classic in its field. Even the random thoughts assembled at the end, which he lacked time to polish and properly organize, help to enhance the reputation of this significant book.

It was also during these last months that Bastiat wrote the famous pamphlet, "What Is Seen and What Is Not Seen." Tragically, Bastiat had lost the entire manuscript during a period when he was relocating his household. After a careful but unsuccessful search, he decided that the pamphlet was of such importance that it deserved being done again. This second manuscript did not suit him, and he threw it into the fire. So, he wrote "What Is Seen and What Is Not Seen" for yet a third time, and this is the form in which we know that classic. In these last days, Bastiat was also thinking ahead to a third series of economic sophisms. When one considers the work accomplished during this period and the ideas which flooded his mind, the question grows: What might this man have done had he been granted more time?

To his old friend Richard Cobden, in August 1850, Bastiat wrote of his literary plans and his physical infirmities:

> I went to my native country to try to cure these unfortunate lungs, which are to me very capricious servants. I have returned a little better, but afflicted with a disease of the larynx, accompanied with a complete extinction of voice. The doctor enjoins absolute silence; and, in consequence, I am about to pass two months in the country, near Paris.

He went on to tell Cobden some of his ideas for the second volume of *Economic Harmonies*. He also outlined another exciting idea which he never lived to develop:

An important task for political economy is to write the history of plunder. It is a long history involving, from the very beginning, conquests, migrations of peoples, invasions, and all the disastrous excesses of violence at grips with justice. All this has left an aftermath that still continues to plague us and that renders it more difficult to solve the problems of the present day. We shall not solve them so long as we are unaware of the way, and of the extent to which, injustice, present in our very midst, has gained a foothold in our customs and laws.

In these last days, sadness piled upon sadness for Bastiat. There had been a death in his family during his absence, he was now totally without political influence, no serious attention had been given to his most recent *Economic Harmonies,* and he was far too ill to fight back. A trip to the Pyrenees, a trip which had improved his bodily spirits several times in the past, this time only aggravated his illness. The infection which had spread to his throat caused his voice to weaken, and began to disturb his digestion as well as his breathing.

In the fall of 1850, Bastiat was sent to Italy by his doctors. Arriving in Pisa, he read in the papers an announcement of his own death. Typically, he was amused at the references to "the great economist" and "the illustrious author." Writing to a friend to contradict the report, he said, "Thank God I am not dead, or even much worse. And yet if the news were true, I must just accept it and submit. I wish all my friends could acquire in this respect the philosophy I have myself acquired. I assure you I should breathe my last without pain, and almost with joy, if I were certain of leaving to the friends who love me, not poignant regrets, but a gentle, affectionate, somewhat melancholy remembrance of me."

From Pisa, Bastiat went on to Rome. Writing his old and

dear friend Coudroy for the last time, Bastiat discussed his plans for writing the second volume of *Economic Harmonies.* In his letter, he continued:

> Here I am in the Eternal City, but not much disposed to visit its marvels. I am infinitely better than I was at Pisa, surrounded as I am with excellent friends. . . . I should desire only one thing, to be relieved of the acute pain which the disease of the windpipe occasions. This continuity of suffering torments me. Every meal is a punishment. To eat, drink, speak, cough, are all painful operations. Walking fatigues me—carriage airings irritate the throat—I can no longer work, or even read, seriously. You see to what I am reduced. I shall soon be little better than a dead body, retaining only the faculty of suffering.

And yet his mind continued to work on plans for the second volume of *Economic Harmonies.*

By Christmas eve of 1850, Bastiat could go on no longer. At the last, he beckoned to those with him to approach the bedside. One of those present reported that ". . . his eye sparkled with that peculiar expression which I had frequently noticed in our conversations, and which announced the solution of a problem." Bastiat raised his head a bit as though to convey something of importance, and twice murmured the words, "The Truth." Then he was gone. Apparently Bastiat had solved one final problem to his satisfaction.

Some months before, Bastiat had written, "What gives me courage is . . . the thought that, perhaps, my life may not have been useless to mankind." For a man who had only been engaged in active public life for some six years, the balance sheet is indeed impressive. He had produced seven volumes of work, together with his service as a major political, social, and economic commentator on his times. While he died too soon to realize that his ideas would have a lasting impact, the seeds he had sown would one day bear fruit. Bastiat's rediscovery in twentieth-century America, a time, and a place plagued by the same false ideas which so plagued his France, is a clear indication that he has had a great impact, perhaps a greater impact than we can yet appreciate.

CHAPTER 8

Bastiat and the Social Architects

I still cannot understand why the numerous partisans of the systems opposed to liberty allow the word *liberty* to remain on the flag of the Republic.

FREDERIC BASTIAT WAS FAR MORE THAN AN ECONOMIC journalist. In his work there appears a grasp of the broadest social issues. In a modern world dominated largely by systems builders, Bastiat has a great deal of importance as an antidote to the subtle poison contained in the idea that some social architects can mold the lives of men to the advantage of all.

Perhaps we should not be surprised that the nineteenth century spawned an unusually large number of social architects. The enormous changes of the Industrial Revolution, coupled with the political revolution which had begun in France and which had swept through country after country in the Western world, had strongly impressed the idea of change upon the European mind. Since that change was not only sweeping in nature, but was, presumably, change for the better, the idea of social reconstruction, of remodeling society in the aftermath of revolution, came to dominate the minds of many. The idea of evolution, so dear to nineteenth-century thinkers, also played its part in promoting the idea of progress. Nineteenth-century thinkers tended to see themselves living between the old and the new, groping toward radical change, toward a new society, toward a new world. Men had flirted with the idea of "progress" since the time of the Greeks, but it was the men of the nineteenth century who promoted progress into the be-all and end-all of society.

The rise of a new industrial working class channeled much of the century's thinking into the confining intellectual framework of socialism. Building upon the anti-individualistic doctrines of Rousseau and the eighteenth-century *philosophes,* the social architects came to feel that only collective and class-oriented action on the part of the workers could produce the "progress" which they felt awaited a properly planned society. Before the theorists were through, they had produced the bloody revolutions of 1848. Marx, in the same year, spelled out the doctrine of class struggle in the *Communist Manifesto,* urging violence as not only necessary but desirable. For most of the other social architects of Marx's generation, the course of action was far less clear. As one distinguished analyst of the period, Louis Baudin, summarizes the era:

> 1840 to 1850 was such a characteristic era that history has given it a name: "the forty years." The storms of the Revolution and the Empire had calmed leaving some dangerous backwaters. Royalty was fading with dignity, the republic was not solidly built up and could not involve itself in the troubles and the ephemerals. Political parties mixed and battled furiously, the overthrown social classes searched for themselves among the debris of the divided and declining nobility. A new bourgeoisie, full of initiative and eager for a profit, took shape, while a miserable and unsettled proletariat was born to a time of industrial revolution. . . .

> The impartial observer has some difficulty finding himself in this
> storm. Excessiveness is the rule; the most absurd political theories find
> defenders, the most audacious politicians have their partisans. More
> passion than wisdom, more swagger than science, more flash than
> solidarity, many words, much protest, agitation, a grand romantic
> gust are the order of the day . . . They [the social architects] sputtered
> words of promise and vague meanings: progress, socialism, sover-
> eignty of the people.

The social architects had been at their work since the eighteenth century. Rousseau, the theorists of the French Revolution, Saint-Simon and Fourier, all these and others had paved
the way for the social theorists who would disrupt France in
the 1840s. Considerant, Blanc, and Proudhon were well prepared to wage war on the social order, all in the name of
Progress.

Bastiat's Style in Controversy

Bastiat recognized, far sooner than most men, the extreme
dangers involved in the new politics and economics. Bastiat
stood on particularly difficult ground since he could not pose
as a defender of the old system under the French monarchy.
In fact, Bastiat was a sharp critic of the old-style interventions
in the lives of men, but he was also perceptive enough to see
that the new-style interventions in the lives of men were an
aggravation to social problems rather than an answer. Thus,
Bastiat was forced to believe in progress. He could not urge a
return to an earlier, happier day and had to meet the social
architects on their own ground, granting their premise of an
unfortunate past and yet pointing out the fallacies involved in
their proposed utopias. In this struggle, Bastiat found himself
cast in a familiar role: a man alone.

Fortunately, Frederic Bastiat brought to his difficult task

both insight and humor. He was also unfailingly fair in his observations. Indeed, Bastiat's good humor and complete fairness in public controversy drove his opponents to distraction. It seems that there is nothing more frustrating than good humor and fair play for the embittered ideologue who is willing to distort the truth in the name of his mission to serve mankind.

Bastiat's good humor and sense of fair play did not render him in any way unable to speak the truth in the most trenchant manner. He called a spade a spade, plainly and frankly. Again and again he challenged the moral basis from which the social architects presumed to control the lives of other men. Bastiat directed his shafts at any and all who would manipulate society. In public debate, in books, in the press, Bastiat time after time crossed swords with virtually all of the prominent political and social thinkers of his time. In the process, he left a legacy of criticism which applies to the social architects of all times.

The Desire for Power

Bastiat probed the minds of the social architects and called attention to the almost total disagreement to be found among them:

> If I had to point out the characteristic trait that differentiates socialism from [a proper view of political economy], I should find it here. Socialism includes a countless number of sects. Each one has its own utopia, and we may well say that they are so far from agreement that they wage bitter war upon one another. Between M. Blanc's *organized social workshops* and M. Proudhon's *anarchy,* between Fourier's *association* and M. Cabet's *communism,* there is certainly all the difference between night and day. What then, is the common denominator to which all forms of socialism are reducible, and what is the bond that unites them against natural society, or society as planned by Providence? There is none except this: *They do not want natural*

society. What they do want is an artificial society, which has come forth full-grown from the brain of its inventor . . . They quarrel over who will mold the human clay, but they agree that there is human clay to mold. Mankind is not in their eyes a living and harmonious being endowed by God Himself with the power to progress and to survive, but an inert mass that has been waiting for them to give it feeling and life; human nature is not a subject to be studied, but matter on which to perform experiments.

It was the recognition of that common trait of the social architects which caused Bastiat to mutter, "I still cannot understand why the numerous partisans of the systems opposed to liberty allow the word *liberty* to remain on the flag of the Republic."

Building upon his observation that the concern of the socialist was the development of an artificial social order, Bastiat stressed the point that the denial of the idea of a natural social order carried with it the denial that man's interests are fundamentally in harmony. Therefore, one of the prerequisites for destroying the natural order of society and substituting an artificial order in its place would be the necessity to demonstrate that men's interests are fundamentally antagonistic, one to another. Thus, the very nature of the social-architect idea necessitated a belief that the property owner and the worker, capital and labor, the common people and the bourgeoisie, agriculture and industry, the farmer and the city dweller, the native born and the foreigner, the producer and the consumer, were all fundamentally in conflict, a conflict which must be furthered until the existing social order was destroyed in the process, thus removing all distinctions between and among men. For Bastiat, this explained how the social architects could profess to be filled to the brim with a love for humanity, yet constantly preach the doctrine of hatred.

The results for France were disastrous; indeed, the results for any country which listens to such prophets of hatred are always the same. Soon the poor rise against the rich, the proletariat against the capitalist, class against class. And when this happens, the social architects then tell us that conflict is the inevitable result of freedom. Substitute social organization and enforced brotherhood and all such conflict will pass away. Thus, those who have engineered our discontent now offer themselves as the only people who know how to bring it to an end.

And how brutal the enforced brotherhood. In the words of the revolutionaries in the France of the 1790's, "Be my brother or I shall kill thee." The social architects preach peace and war, harmony and disharmony, in the same breath, promising absolution from the human condition if we will only listen to them. Bastiat described Napoleon as a chemist who saw in Europe material for his experiment. He made it clear that the French revolutionaries of the 1790's, Napoleon, and the socialists who had followed in the nineteenth century, for all their bitter conflicts with one another, all shared the same essential view. He was fond of pointing out the fundamental contradiction involved:

The demands of the socialists raise another question, which I have often addressed to them, and to which, as far as I know, they have never replied. Since the natural inclinations of mankind are so evil that its liberty must be taken away, how is it that the inclinations of the socialists are good? Are not the legislators and their agents part of the human race? Do they believe themselves molded from another clay than the rest of mankind? They say that society, left to itself, heads inevitably for destruction because its instincts are perverse.

They demand the power to stop mankind from sliding down this fatal
declivity and to impose a better direction on it. If, then, they have
received from heaven intelligence and virtues that place them beyond
and above mankind, let them show their credentials. They want to be
shepherds, and they want us to be their *sheep.* This arrangement
presupposes in them a natural superiority, a claim that we have every
right to require them to establish before we go any further.

Bastiat, of course, knew full well that the excuse of the social
architects for assuming great power was that the power was in
the hands of the state, for the good of all. As a benevolent and
inexhaustible being, the state would provide ". . . bread for all
mouths, work for all hands, capital for all enterprises, credit for
all projects, ointment for all wounds, balm for all suffering,
advice for all perplexities, solutions for all problems, truths for
all minds, distractions for all varieties of boredom, milk for
children and wine for old age," and thus become the agency
". . . which provides for all our needs, foresees all our desires,
satisfies all our curiousity, corrects all our errors, amends all
our faults, and exempts us all henceforth from the need for
foresight, prudence, judgment, sagacity, experience, order,
economy, temperance, and industry." It was Bastiat's great gift
to be able to spell out the assumptions of the social architects
so clearly and simply, leaving the absurdity to speak for itself.

Yet, there lurked behind that absurdity the terrible truth
which lies at the heart of all social planning:

If you start with the already absurd assumption that the government
is the morally active force and that the nation is passive, are you not
putting morals, doctrines, opinions, wealth, everything that makes up
the life of the individual at the mercy of the men who one after another
come to power?

Rousseau

It is possible to discover in Bastiat's published works his analyses of the various fallacies that the social architects have displayed in their positions. Much of considerable import for our time can be gleaned from Bastiat's analyses of Rousseau, the architects of the French Revolution, Saint-Simon and Fourier, and the later social architects contemporary with Bastiat. In his analysis of the family tree of the socialist mentality, he penetrates to the heart of the problem.

Convinced that Jean-Jacques Rousseau was the logical starting point for an analysis of the thinking dominating nineteenth-century France, Bastiat often discussed the eighteenth-century *philosophe* and his work. As he stated frankly in an 1848 article appearing in the *Journal des economistes:*

> Rousseau was convinced that God, nature, and man were wrong. I know that this opinion still sways many minds, but mine is not one of them.

Bastiat was extremely critical of Rousseau's idea that man was born in a state of nature and could only achieve true happiness by returning to that state. As he satirized Rousseau's position, ". . . man's true bliss is to be found in living in the woods, alone, naked, without ties, without affections, without language, without religion, without ideas, without family—in short, in a condition in which he was so little different from the beasts that it is really doubtful whether he stood upright and whether he did not have paws rather than hands." Rousseau, of course, had attacked property and social organization as the great dangers of mankind. For Bastiat, the opposition which Rousseau had set up between the state of nature and the state of society could only result in the denial of all justice and morality. In Rousseau's *Social Contract,* the *philosophe* had pursued the point even further, insisting that violation of the social contract allowed all parties to that contract to return to a state of "natural liberty," completely freed from any and all obligations to the social order. As Bastiat warned, the havoc which such a doctrine would wreak in an age of revolution was incalculable. In fact, the events of the French Revolution following 1789 were ample proof of how disastrous Rousseau's position could be. When Bastiat described the results of Rousseau's position, he was describing a situation of both his time and our own:

> What young man, going out into the world full of ardor and passion, does not say to himself: "The impulses of my heart are the voice of Nature, which is never mistaken. The institutions that stand in my way are man-made and are only arbitrary conventions to which I have never given my consent. In trampling these institutions underfoot, I shall have the double pleasure of satisfying my inclinations and of believing myself a hero."

Bastiat also faulted Rousseau for his insistence upon the *General Will,* a doctrine completely out of harmony with the "state of nature" position. In Rousseau's *General Will,* the future for the entire human race was to be found in subservience to a collective will of all men. The rights of private property and the guarantees of individual personality were to be swept aside and replaced with a collective *We,* operating under the care of the lawgiver, i.e., the social architect. Thus, Rousseau and many social revolutionaries since have said to the population, "Sweep aside all the restraints of property and society, destroy the existing system. Then you will be free, free to lose yourself in the collective good of mankind, under my care." In Bastiat's analysis of Rousseau's *Social Contract,* it is possible to see how a certain mentality can rebel against all authority at one moment arid yet espouse the most total socialist attitudes a moment later:

> Start with the idea that society is contrary to Nature; devise contrivances to which humanity can be subjected; lose sight of the fact that humanity has its motive force within itself; consider men as base raw materials; propose to impart to them movement at will, feeling and life; set oneself up apart, immeasurably above the human race—these are the common practices of the social planners. The plans differ; the planners are all alike . . .

> Poor human race! What would the disciples of Rousseau do to your dignity?

The French Revolutionaries

Bastiat realized that the theoretical contradictions of Rousseau had been borne out in practice by the events of the French Revolution. In 1789, the old regime had been swept aside as repressive, just in time for the leaders of the Revolution to busy themselves in imposing a new and artificially planned society on the French people. Analyzing the words and actions of Saint-Just, Robespierre, and the other revolutionaries, Bastiat made it clear that they were all in agreement concerning the necessity of dictatorship to promote virtue. In Robespierre's words, "The principle of republican government is virtue, and the means needed to establish it is terror." Bastiat spoke for all men in all ages when he analyzed Robespierre:

> At what a height above the rest of mankind Robespierre here places himself! And note the arrogance with which he speaks. He does not confine himself to expressing the wish for a great renovation of the human heart; he does not even expect such a result from a regular

government. No, he wants to bring it to pass himself, and by means of terror . . . Note that when Robespierre demands a dictatorship, it is . . . to make his own moral principles prevail by means of terror. . . . Oh, you wretches! You who believe yourselves so great! You who regard mankind as so inconsiderable! You want to reform everything! Reform yourselves first! This will be enough of a task for you.

Bastiat traced in great detail the assaults upon private property which had characterized the French Revolution. He pointed out that it had thrown aside all of the genuine guarantees of human freedom and personality, substituting the most brutal repressions in their place. He also reminded us that those repressions were invariably carried out in the name of "the people," as though there could be a public good arising from a private wrong.

Saint-Simon and Fourier

The madness begun in the French revolutionary era was destined to be nurtured and expanded in the nineteenth century. The Count Henri de Saint-Simon conceived a plan to make over France as a collectivist economy, under the control of technical experts. He insisted that man must be studied not as an individual, but *en masse,* and that all future social institutions must be organized around the masses. All this was to be done in the name of Christian ethics, as a part of a rather confused system of "the new Christianity." Saint-Simon's disciples were given to the most bizarre ideas and activities. For a time, his followers dressed in a blue tunic with trousers to match and a scarlet jersey which buttoned at the back and which could not be undone except with the aid of some other person. The peculiar and impractical costume was intended to symbolize the mutual dependence of one man upon another.

Such groups would sometimes go from place to place throughout the country, and indeed even toured foreign countries, once reaching Constantinople, in a misbegotten missionary effort to convert the whole world to their new system.

François Fourier developed his own bizarre ideas and followers. For this particular social architect, cooperation was to replace competition as everyone left the exploitive industrial system to return to Rousseau's state of nature on cooperative farms. Though the Phalanxes, as the groups were called, sprang up throughout France and even spread to the United States, they were characterized more by strange ideas and actions than by lasting success.

At least such early utopians as Saint-Simon and Fourier did not feel it necessary to institute a revolutionary bloodbath against those choosing not to follow their direction. But the seeds of madness were present, nonetheless. The later social architects contemporary to Bastiat revealed a new urgency, a bitter impatience, that would one day convulse France in revolutionary outbursts.

"A Marxist before Karl Marx"

Bastiat engaged the social architects of his time individually and collectively. One of his more spectacular battles was his confrontation with Victor Considerant concerning the right of property. Bastiat published an analysis of Considerant's position which drew the ire of the man characterized as "a Marxist before Marx."

Considerant had adopted the position that the right of employment was a right owed by society to all men, a right therefore enforceable by government. Bastiat had pointed out that such a "right" carried with it the threat of the destruction of all private property if government acted upon the notion.

Considerant had posed as a defender of property, as a man wishing to make only a small change in the existing system in order to prevent unrest. He complained that Bastiat was mis-representing his position, that his "right of employment" was only a necessary modification of the system to help it function more efficiently. How familiar that sounds today. Pointing out that an attack upon the property rights of anyone finally amounted to an attack on the property rights of all men, Bastiat insisted that property was an extension of individual personality. Unless such extensions of self were guaranteed against the aggressions of the state, no matter how "humanitarian" those aggressions might be, the position of the individual within society would soon be untenable. Bastiat concluded his public demolition of the Considerant position:

> If, then, M. Considerant is a tenacious defender of property, it is at least of a concept of property different from that which has been recognized and maintained among men since the beginning of the world.
>
> I am quite convinced that M. Louis Blanc and M. Proudhon also call themselves defenders of property as they understand it.

Louis Blanc

Considerably more attractive to the French people, and therefore far more dangerous, were the ideas put forth by Louis Blanc. In a number of newspaper pieces, and in his book, *The Organization of Labor,* Blanc had insisted that the government had an obligation to guarantee employment to all able-bodied men. The idea of collective workshops had originated with him. Unalterably opposed to any form of competition, Blanc believed that his program would avoid the "exploitations" of the new industrial system and would also avoid class warfare.

For this reason, Blanc always fondly supposed that both workers and bourgeoisie would be attracted to his program. He believed that his new workshops would drive all private enterprise out of existence, and that mankind would now be happier in the planned community living which would develop around his workshops. One commentator has suggested that Blanc's bitter hatred of any superiority and his absolute insistence upon virtual equality of all men may have stemmed from some psychological need to assert himself the equal of all men, since, in physical stature, Louis Blanc was a dwarf.

Of all the ruthless leaders in mid-century France, Louis Blanc was perhaps most popular, in part because his ideas were readily understandable and were contained within the simple slogan, "the right to employment." His popularity further rested on his reputation as an outspoken jingo. He urged a militant foreign policy on France to perpetuate the glories of the Napoleonic era. The discipline of the National Workshops and the discipline of the national armies apparently served a common purpose for Blanc.

Again and again, Blanc and Bastiat crossed swords. Each time, the specious arguments of Blanc suffered in the transaction:

Do you not know that freedom means competition, and that competition, according to M. Louis Blanc, is *a system of extermination for the common people, and a cause of ruin for the businessman?* For evidence that the freer nations are, the closer they are to destruction and ruination, should we not look at Switzerland, Holland, England, and the United States [then easily the four most prosperous nations on earth]? Do you not know that, again according to M. Louis Blanc, *competition leads to monopoly,* and that, *for the same reason, low costs lead to high prices? That competition tends to exhaust the sources of comsumption and pushes production into a destructive activity? That competition forces production to increase and consumption to decrease?* Whence it follows that free peoples produce in order not to consume

—that liberty *means both oppression and madness,* and that M. Louis
Blanc simply must step in and set matters straight?

Proudhon

Another of the social architects, Pierre Joseph Proudhon, is
best known for his denunciation of private property as theft.
His theories tend to run the gambit of nineteenth-century politics, so much so that he has been variously classified as both
a philosophic anarchist and as a forerunner of fascism. Proudhon had no patience with the more popular Louis Blanc, and
even less patience with those who quoted "property is theft"
by removing the remark from its full context. Proudhon was
probably less radical than some of his fellow social planners.
In fact, he preferred the American system in operation during
the first half of the nineteenth century precisely because it
governed least. For French politics, whether monarchical or
republican, Proudhon had nothing but contempt. He suspected
that the Louis Blancs of this world were little better than
demagogues, and did not hesitate to say so.

At first glance, Proudhon might seem almost a sufficient
maverick to stand with Bastiat against the currents of his time.
However, Proudhon was so radical in his assumptions, and so
quick to change his viewpoint, that some of his most bitter
invective was reserved for controversy with Bastiat. When
these two worthy antagonists met in the pages of the Paris
newspapers, the clash resounded throughout France. The famous debate between the two men was first printed in the
columns of Proudhon's paper, *The Voice of the People,* during
1849. Each man wrote one letter a week for twelve weeks.
Proudhon's temper, never noted for stability, soon drove him
beyond the bounds of polite discourse. Answering one of Bastiat's letters, Proudhon wrote:

> Your intelligence sleeps, or rather it has never been awake. . . . You are a man for whom logic does not exist. . . . You do not hear anything, you do not understand anything. . . . You are without philosophy, without science, without humanity. . . . Your ability to reason, like your ability to pay attention and to make comparisons, is zero. . . . Scientifically, Mr. Bastiat, you are a dead man.

Proudhon's ill temper doubtless was provoked by the sound and persistent analysis which Bastiat brought to the debate. Most of the published debate had centered on the moral, legal, and economic justifications for the taking of interest. Bastiat, of course, defended the principle; Proudhon attacked it. Philosophically, Bastiat probably had the better of the debate. He certainly had the practical satisfaction of seeing Proudhon's "Bank of the People" (featuring cooperative exchange of goods and services, as well as interest-free loans) fail in 1849.

It should not be surprising that a classical liberal like Bastiat and an anarchist like Proudhon should agree on many points. But Proudhon saw paradox everywhere and could agree with no one for long. Bastiat regarded him as one of the dangerous men of the times:

> In recent times great pains have been taken to stir up public resentment against that infamous, that diabolical thing, capital. It is pictured to the masses as a ravenous and insatiable monster, more deadly than cholera, more terrifying than riots, as a vampire whose insatiable appetite is fed by more and more of the life-blood of the body politic. The tongue of this blood-sucking monster is called "rent," "usury," "hire," "service charges," "interest." A writer whose great talents could have made him famous had he not preferred to use them to coin the paradoxes that have brought him notoriety has seen fit to cast this paradox before a people already tormented by the fever of revolution.

Proudhon prided himself on the "discovery" that contradiction lies at the heart of all phenomena, that all institutions and ideas are hopelessly contradictory. Bastiat was sharply critical of that quality in Proudhon's thought and public behavior:

> God, a contradiction; liberty, a contradiction; property, a contradiction; value, credit, monopoly, common ownership, contradiction on contradiction! When M. Proudhon made this tremendous discovery, his heart must surely have leaped for joy; for since contradiction is in all things, there is always something to contradict, which for him is the supreme happiness. He once said to me, "I'd be perfectly willing to go to heaven, but I'm afraid that everybody agrees up there, and I couldn't find anyone to argue with."

Bastiat warned that such men as Proudhon, who were introducing doubts about the function of capital into the minds of French workers, were doing irreparable harm. Bastiat pointed out again and again that the progress of humanity coincided with the rapid formation of capital; he insisted that capital could not increase unless society were allowed to grow, and unless savings and security were possible:

> We can hardly exert direct action on the energy and frugality of our fellow men, except through public opinion, through an intelligent expression of our likes and our dislikes. But we can do a great deal for the creation of security, without which capital, far from expanding, goes into hiding, takes flight, or is destroyed; and consequently we see how almost suicidal is the ardor for disturbing the public peace that the working classes sometimes display. They must learn that capital has from the beginning of time worked to free men from the yoke of ignorance, want, and tyranny. To frighten away capital is to rivet a triple chain around the arms of the human race.

Bastiat suggested that workers and capitalists must cease to look at one another with envy and distrust. He suggested that they turn from the demagogic tirades to which they were constantly subjected and recognize that their interests were common and identical. Bastiat reminded his readers that capital made possible all social advance:

> Thus, no matter what our point of view, whether we consider capital in its relation to our wants, which it ennobles; to our satisfactions, which it refines; to Nature, which it tames for us; to morality, which it makes habitual in us; to our social consciousness, which it develops; to equality, which it fosters; to liberty, which is its life-blood; to justice, which it guarantees by the most ingenious methods; we shall perceive always and everywhere (provided only that it be created and put to work in a social order that has not been diverted from its natural course) that capital bears that seal and hallmark of all the great laws of Providence: harmony.

Having defended capital and property against all the slurs and misunderstandings common to mid-nineteenth-century France, and having pointed out that the fullest possible guarantee for the property rights of all was the best possible means to achieve the capital formation necessary for the advance of society, Bastiat leveled one final attack against Proudhon and his ideas:

> We must cease believing in anything in this world, in facts, in justice, in universal consent, in human language; or else we must admit that these two words, "property" and "plunder," express opposite, irreconcilable ideas that can no more be identified than yes and no, light and dark, good and evil, harmony and discord. Taken literally, the famous formula, *property is theft,* is therefore absurdity raised to the nth degree. It would be no less outlandish to say that *theft is property;* that what is legal is illegal; that what is, is not, etc.

Bastiat went on to agree with Proudhon that some men were paid for work they did not do, thus appropriating the property of others. However, the proper description of such plunder should not be *property is theft,* but *theft is theft.* Such theft, or plunder, could only be stopped when men realized that property must be kept sacred and inviolable from the assaults of all aggressions, public or private.

The Future of France

In Bastiat's day as in our own, the majority of the legislators of his country did not regard themselves as socialists, yet France was deeply involved in a socialistic course of action. On more than one occasion, Bastiat asked himself, "Why?" He knew that the amount of government action increased and decreased in various countries and in various periods of history. Bastiat took Sparta as a model of perfect political oppression, and the United States as the closest approach to a truly free society, regarding France as a mid-point between the United States and Sparta. Bastiat warned Frenchmen that men could have freedom or could have the "security" of being unfree, but that no attempted mixture of the two could long prevail. In a society in which coercion was rampant, soon nothing but coercion would exist. But so long as men believed that the state could provide more than universal justice, so long as political power was used in an attempt to satisfy the wants of society, coercion would always be rampant, and justice impossible, whether or not the leaders of a country regarded themselves as socialists.

Looking back over four major revolutions practically within his own lifetime, Bastiat pointed out that this unrest and dis-

ruption must inevitably follow the attempt of the state to perform functions which it could not possibly fulfill. And he never
tired of restating the fundamental premise for an orderly and
prosperous society:

> Property is prior to law; the sole function of the law is to safeguard
> the right to property wherever it exists, wherever it is formed, in
> whatever manner the worker produces it, whether individually or in
> association, provided that he respects the rights of others.

In contrast with that simple definition of justice and prosperity, Bastiat described the France of his time:

> Why do our legislators thus contravene all sound notions of political
> economy? Why do they not leave things in their proper place: altruism
> in its natural realm, which is liberty; and justice in its, which is law?
> Why do they not use the law exclusively to further justice? It is not
> that they do not love justice, but that they have no confidence in it.
> Justice is liberty and property. But they are socialists without know-
> ing it; for achieving the progressive reduction of poverty and the
> progressive increase in wealth, they have no faith, whatever they may
> say, in liberty or in property or, consequently, in justice. And that is
> why we see them in all good faith seeking to achieve the good by the
> constant violation of the right.

From long experience, Bastiat knew what response would be
made to such a plea. He knew that inequality, distress, and
suffering daily presented themselves to the eyes of all concerned
Frenchmen, and he knew that such inequality would be assumed to be a failing brought about by insufficient government
intervention in redressing the balance of society. He well knew,
however, that France suffered, not from too little government,

but from too much. He pointed out that the advocates of intervention had promised many benefits and no taxes to the people. Of course, the government could not possibly fulfill such a promise, leaving itself open to the cries of demagogues: "Those in power are deceiving you; if we were in their place, we would overwhelm you with benefits and free you from all taxes." Four times in scarcely more than fifty years the French people had responded to such a cry with revolution. Of course, the new government could no more provide justice by unjust means, prosperity by destroying property, or morality by immoral actions than could the previous government. Thus, the people were doomed to endless disappointment and French society to continuing injustice, inequality, and terrible economic and political distress.

Such a system was bound to grow continually worse, for it relied upon more intervention in the lives of its citizens to deal with problems originally caused by intervention! When the communists cried for equality, Bastiat correctly predicted the result:

> ... on what basis will the distribution be made? Communism answers: On the basis of equality. What! Equality without reference to any difference in pains taken? We shall all have an equal *share,* whether we have worked six hours or twelve, mechanically or intellectually! But of all possible types of inequality this is the most shocking; and furthermore, it means the destruction of all initiative, liberty, dignity, and prudence. You propose to kill competition, but take care; you are only redirecting it. Under present conditions we compete to see who works most and best. Under your regime we shall compete to see who works worst and least.

Bastiat also foretold that the expansion of public services would inevitably lead to the destruction of private services:

But when private services become public, they are exempt from competition, and this admirable harmony is no longer manifested. The public official, in fact, is deprived of the stimulus that urges us on to progress. And how can progress work for the common good when it is nonexistent? The civil servant acts, not under the spur of self-interest, but under the shadow of the law. The law says to him: "You will render the public a certain fixed service, and you will receive from the public a certain other fixed service in return." A little more or a little less zeal changes nothing in these fixed terms. Self-interest, on the other hand, whispers these words into the ear of the free worker: "The more you do for others, the more others will do for you."

Once injustice is organized into a system which takes from one man to give to another, the resultant distortions spread throughout society. Capital becomes frightened, credit takes flight, work is suspended. Why produce when one is not allowed to keep the fruits of that production. In Bastiat's time, such sentiment was spreading rapidly throughout the bourgeoisie. The great specter of the times was *communism*. But Bastiat reminded the bourgeoisie that exactly the same principle of taking from one to give to another by means of government force had already been practiced in the tariff and other measures favoring the middle class. All that was now being done was extending the same principle to the lower classes as well. Bastiat was quick to tell the middle classes that they had paved the way for their own destruction. And yet, the further society moved in the direction of "redressing injustices" the worse the situation was likely to become:

Capital and labor will be frightened; they will no longer be able to count on the future. Capital, under the impact of such a doctrine, will hide, flee, be destroyed. And what will become, then, of the workers, those workers for whom you profess an affection so deep and sincere, but so enlightened? Will they be better fed when agricultural production is stopped? Will they be better dressed when no one dares to build

a factory? Will they have more employment when capital will have
disappeared?

Bastiat recognized that such a day was fast approaching in
France, and indeed would be fast approaching in any society
which did not secure the property and freedom of the individual.

The Moral Corruptions of the Interventionist State

While the material price for interventionism was thus predicta-
bly high, Bastiat always stressed that the moral price demanded by the interventionist state was even higher. Drawing
upon the experiences of 1848, he pointed out that the entire
population of France, particularly the poor, had been led to
believe that government could somehow satisfy all their needs
and desires. A great "war on poverty" had been promised the
French people. Bastiat warned that the government could not
possibly alleviate poverty, since it was government intervention
which had caused the hardships:

> Take from some to give to others! I know that this is the way things
> have been going for a long time. But, before contriving, in our effort
> to banish poverty, various means of putting this outlandish principle
> into effect, ought we not rather to ask ourselves whether poverty is
> not due to the very fact that this principle has already been put into
> effect in one way or another? Before seeking the remedy in the further
> disturbance of the natural law of society, ought we not first to make
> sure that these disturbances are not themselves the very cause of the
> social ills that we wish to cure?"

Bastiat recognized that a great political revolution had taken
place which had given all power into the hands of "the people."

He warned that the precedent had already been too well established by the upper classes of feathering their own nests at the expense of others. Such ideas were sure to spread to the lower classes, producing the ugly spectacle of a society in which everyone was attempting to live at the expense of everyone else. Soon all classes demand special privileges. In the absurd rhetoric of the socialist demagogue, such a system is presumably fraternal and egalitarian, with total justice for all concerned:

> And is not this the point that we have now reached? What is the cry going up everywhere, from all ranks and classes? *All for one!* When we say the word *one* we think of ourselves, and what we demand is to receive an unearned share in the fruits of the labor of all. In other words, we are creating an organized system of plunder. Unquestionably, simple out-and-out plunder is so clearly unjust as to be repugnant to us; but thanks to the motto, *all for one,* we can allay our qualms of conscience. We impose on others the *duty* of working for us. Then, we arrogate to ourselves the *right* to enjoy the fruits of other men's labor. We call upon the state, the law, to enforce our so-called *duty,* to protect our so-called *right,* and we end in the fantastic situation of robbing one another in the name of brotherhood. We live at other men's expense, and then call ourselves heroically self-sacrificing for so doing. Oh, the unaccountable folly of the human mind! Oh, the deviousness of greed! It is not enough that each of us tries to increase our share at the expense of others; it is not enough that we want to profit from labor that we have not performed. We even convince ourselves that in the process we are sublime examples of self-sacrifice; we almost go so far as to call our unselfishness Christlike. We have become so blind that we do not see that the sacrifices that cause us to weep with admiration as we contemplate ourselves are not made by us at all, but are exacted by us of others.

Such a society which loses all sense of justice or morality is likely to court disaster by rushing further and further in the wrong direction. Once people come to believe it both possible and just for government to take from others to provide their livelihood, the nature of government is such that it will hasten to multiply the number of jobs at its disposal, to extend its patronage, to swell in importance in an inevitable process of empire building. Once the empire is built upon such false premises, the corruption will spread by leaps and bounds through both the governors and the governed:

> . . . what will happen to the morality of the institution when its treasury is fed by taxes; when no one, except possibly some bureaucrat, finds it to his interest to defend the common fund; when every member, instead of making it his duty to prevent abuses, delights in encouraging them; when all mutual supervision has stopped, and malingering becomes merely a good trick played on the government? The government, to give it its just due, will be disposed to defend itself; but, no longer being able to count on private action, will have to resort to official action. It will appoint various agents, examiners, controllers, and inspectors. It will set up countless formalities as barriers between the workers' claims and his relief payments. In a word, an admirable institution will, from its very inception, be turned into a branch of the police force.

Thus Frederic Bastiat predicted the end result of a war on poverty fought by political means. Over 100 years ago he quite clearly saw a truth which modern society is only beginning to appreciate.

Bastiat realized that unless men are allowed to experiment, to choose, to make mistakes and pay for them, make proper decisions and be rewarded by them, in short, to act for themselves on their own responsibility, they are denied precisely that quality of free choice which makes them men. The individual who is relieved of responsibility for his own actions incurs the gravest possible handicap for the future development of his own personality. Soon such men find no capacity in themselves, and turn to government for the solution of all problems:

> . . . the citizens have lost their capacity for initiative. At the very instant that they are about to regain the liberty that they have so ardently pursued, they become frightened; they reject it. Do you offer them the freedom to provide their own education? They fear that all learning will be lost. Do you offer them freedom of worship? They fear that atheism will make inroads everywhere. They have been told so many times that all religion, all wisdom, all knowledge, all enlightenment, all morality reside in the state or are derived from the state!

The failures of such a system inevitably lead to public unrest, to demonstrations in the street, to cries urging overthrow of the existing regime. France had repeatedly undergone such a process, and public disorder had become the rule rather than the exception. Some men urged that such revolution would correct the abuses; Bastiat knew better, accurately prophesying the direction which "anti-establishment" agitation would take in a socialized society:

> I cannot refrain from observing that, when things are organized in this way, when the government, by turning one free and voluntary transaction after another into a public service, has come to assume gigantic proportions, there is reason to fear that revolutions, which are in themselves so great an evil, will cease even to have the advantage of being a remedy, except by dint of repeated experience. The loss of responsibility has perverted public opinion. The people, accustomed to calling upon the state for everything, accuse the government, not of doing too much, but of not doing enough. They overthrow it and replace it by another, to which they do not say: *Do less,* but: *Do more;* and thus the abyss that yawns before us becomes ever deeper.

The Natural Development of Society

The way ahead which Bastiat offered as an alternative to the blind alley into which France had stumbled was simplicity itself: the condition of freedom. He recognized that freedom produced harmony, since the natural ordering of society carried with it the possibility of true justice. If men were left free to pursue their own devices, if force were once and for all removed from the everyday productive life of the individual, society could indeed be harmonious. He admitted that the France of his time lacked leadership to achieve such a noble goal:

> . . . unfortunately, it was impossible for the National Assembly to follow this course or to speak these words. These utterances were not in accord with the Assembly's thinking or with the public's expectations. . . . Be responsible for ourselves! they would have said. Look to the state for nothing beyond law and order! Count on it for no wealth, no enlightenment! No more holding it responsible for our faults, our negligence, our improvidence! Count only on ourselves for our subsistence, our physical, intellectual, and moral progress! Merciful heavens! What is going to become of us? Won't society give way to poverty, ignorance, error, irreligion, and perversity?

Bastiat understood more clearly than any other man of his time the painful lesson that societies will never change for the better until the individuals composing that society come to understand fully their own moral responsibilities. Once enough men fully perceive that responsibility and thereby release the productive energies which come from full development of that responsibility, we will have both a moral and a prosperous society. Meanwhile, the schemes of the social architects will continue to lead us astray.

CHAPTER 9

Conservatives and Libertarians

To tamper with man's freedom is not only to injure him, to
degrade him; it is to change his nature, to render him, in so far
as such oppression is exercised, incapable of improvement; it is
to strip him of his resemblance to the Creator, to stifle within
him the noble breath of life with which he was endowed at his
creation.

WITHIN AMERICAN SOCIETY, THE ENORMOUS AUTHORITY OF
the modern state has produced the reaction which inevitably
occurs when power becomes super-centralized. Thirty years
ago, that reaction consisted primarily in being *against* big
government, with no very clear definition of what should be put
in its place. Over the ensuing years, however, foes of big government, those in opposition to the strange amalgam of ideas
generally called "liberalism," have gradually evolved a height-
ened awareness of the philosophic basis for such opposition.

We might better say philosophic bases, since there are *two*
basic positions which have evolved. The political shorthand of
our times has labeled them *conservative* and *libertarian.* As is
usually the case with political shorthand, no one knows with
certainty what these terms mean. At best, they describe only
a general tendency rather than a precise position. Most conservatives are libertarian in their concern over the expansion of
governmental authority into the lives of individuals. Most

libertarians are conservative in the sense that they draw upon an old and established tradition of limited government and individual dignity stemming from both the American experience and the broader experience held in common by the Western world.

Such breadth of definition sometimes allows dreadful misuse of the terms. If we are to believe some commentators, fascists are conservatives, and pornographers are libertarians. The resultant semantic chaos has done much to confuse and discredit the intellectual position of those who value the concepts of the individual, private property, and limited government.

This subject deserves discussion in an examination of Frederic Bastiat's life because he lived through the transitional period during which the ideas constituting today's conservative and libertarian positions were being developed. As an ardent foe of big government, he at once observed and contributed to the arguments for freedom. In him, we can see the fruits of the Whig tradition which had been long developing in England. In the French and English political events of his time, we can perceive the seeds of corruption which were soon to sprout in liberalism, converting a freedom philosophy into a collection of ideas almost totally interventionist in nature.

In Bastiat's reaction to the thinking of his time, we see a man drawing upon the thoughts of some of his predecessors, while projecting ideas which others would use later in the nineteenth century. Locke, Smith, Burke, Coleridge, Bentham, Mill— these and others are echoed or anticipated in Bastiat. Thus Bastiat forms a vital link in our understanding of the strengths and weaknesses contained in the philosophy which men offer in opposition to the omnipotent state.

The only means of penetrating the twisted trail of "conservative-libertarian" thought as reflected in Bastiat is a consideration of several generations of British and French thinkers. Such an examination of one's intellectual forebears is well worth the effort, though it is unlikely to provide the simplistic answers so beloved of all doctrinaires, whether "Liberal," "Conservative," or "Libertarian." Indeed one of the strongest arguments of those who value freedom is the insistent idea that human endeavor cannot be encompassed within *any* philosophy which divorces itself from reality, no matter whose it might be. A bit of complexity may be good for the soul. Be that as it may, it is absolutely essential to an understanding of Frederic Bastiat and his significance.

The Whig Tradition

By far the most effective treatment of the Whig tradition in history appears in Friedrich Hayek's *The Constitution of Liberty*. Hayek traces the development of the Whig emphasis upon individual liberty to seventeenth-century England, where the new emphasis upon freedom appeared more as the "by-product of a struggle for power rather than as the result of deliberate aim." He credits the Middle Ages for their contribution to the idea of freedom, but looks primarily to the Glorious Revolution of 1688 and to John Locke's speculations about the philosophical foundations of government as the real source of the Whig tradition:

> While in his philosophical discussion Locke's concern is with the source which makes power legitimate and with the aim of government in general, the practical problem with which he is concerned is how power, whoever exercises it, can be prevented from becoming arbitrary: "Freedom of men under government is to have a standing rule to live by, common to every one of that society, and made by the legislative power erected in it; a liberty to follow my own will in all things, where that rule prescribes not: and not to be subject to the

inconstant, uncertain, arbitrary will of another man." It is against the "irregular and uncertain exercise of the power" that the argument is mainly directed: the important point is that "whoever has the legislative or supreme power of any commonwealth is bound to govern by established standing laws promulgated and known to the people, and not by extemporary decrees; by indifferent and upright judges, who are to decide controversies by those laws; and to employ the forces of the community at home only in the execution of such laws." Even the legislature has no "absolute arbitrary power," "cannot assume to itself a power to rule by extemporary arbitrary decrees, but is bound to dispense justice, and decide the rights of the subject by promulgated standing laws, and known authorized judges," while the "supreme executor of the law . . . has no will, no power but that of the law . . . his ultimate aim throughout is what today is often called the "taming of power": the end why men "choose and authorize a legislative is that there may be laws made, and rules set, as guards and fences to the properties of all the members of society, to limit the power and moderate the dominion of every part and member of that society."

However much the Whig ideas of John Locke had gained popular acceptance by the beginning of the eighteenth century, it is in the development of public policy in eighteenth-century England that we see the ideas gradually put into effect. The Whigs increasingly implemented a system of limited government favorable to individual liberty, described in Hayek's *The Road to Serfdom* as "The Rule of Law." The Whigs were never very explicit in the delineation of their ideas. Something in the empirical and non-doctrinaire British mind mitigated against any precise formulation. Perhaps the Whig position could best be described as an attempt to free men from the caprices of political control. Again in Hayek's words:

Later in the century [Eighteenth] these ideals are more often taken for granted than explicitly stated, and the modern reader has to infer them when he wants to understand what men like Adam Smith and his contemporaries meant by "liberty." Only occasionally, as in

Blackstone's *Commentaries,* do we find endeavors to elaborate particular points, such as the significance of the independence of the judges
and of the separation of powers, or to clarify the meaning of "law"
by its definition as "a rule, not a transient sudden order from a
superior or concerning a particular person; but something permanent,
uniform and universal."

Edmund Burke

Though Whigs such as Adam Smith did not spell out in detail
what they meant by "liberty," there can be little doubt that
their thinking was strongly oriented toward individual freedom, as protected by "The Rule of Law." Certainly in the work
of Edmund Burke the tradition is given a statement which is
unmistakable. Burke was writing in response to the events of
the French Revolution. He saw the events following 1789 as a
violent overthrow of all the guarantees of private property and
individual liberty upon which the Whig tradition was based.
Burke is generally regarded as the founder of modern conservatism since he resisted the rationalist contempt for the past and
enunciated the necessity for strong and deep ties with tradition.
He spoke for the aristocratic and freedom-oriented Whig land
owners of his time. *Reflections on the Revolution in France* was
published in 1790. From beginning to end it is a ringing indict-
ment of the rationalist position. Burke savagely attacked the
idea that men could generate a perfect society through some
mad scheme which would overturn all existing order. He spoke
as strongly against the social architects of his day as Bastiat did
in France five decades later.

Edmund Burke saw the Whig Revolution of 1688 as "a
revolution not made, but prevented," describing the revolution
which overthrew James II as an attempt to preserve the institutions, laws, and liberties of England, with its traditional con-

cerns for the individual and for the guarantees for private property. He contrasted the Whig Revolution of 1688 with the French Revolution of 1789 and its resultant destruction, terror, and anarchy.

Earlier, Burke had been sympathetic to the American Revolution of 1776, which he described as an attempt to preserve the rights of property and the freedoms of individuals against the attacks of government. In fact, Burke and many of the distinguished Whigs of his time had spoken up in defense of the American Revolution during the critical years when the colonies were winning their independence.

Burke and the Whigs had also consistently championed the liberties of the mind. In speech after speech before Parliament, Burke had defended freedom of speech (1771), religious freedom (1773), and all guarantees of individual action against the overweening power of government. In Burke, the essentially libertarian nature of modern conservatism at its best is readily apparent.

Frenchmen and Englishmen

Burke's reaction to the French Revolution crystalized two views of human freedom and the means to its attainment. The British view, unsystematic and based upon the preservation of past traditions and institutions of freedom, is clearly at odds with the French view, which is rationalist, given to flattering presuppositions about the perfectibility of human nature, and prone to the construction of utopian societies. The English school of thought can be seen quite clearly in the Whigs, Adam Smith, and Edmund Burke. The French *philosophes* and Physiocrats epitomize the French tradition. It should be emphasized that men on both sides of the Channel believed in human freedom; it was in their underlying philosophic assumptions that the enormous differences lay. If the British tradition would honor the past, the French would sweep it away in a torrent of change. If the French would construct a utopia, the English would distrust all closet philosophies not hammered out on the anvil of experience. If the English tradition would take human nature as it found it, the French would assume that man was perfectible. If the French were prone to speak of Man, the English preferred to speak of individual men, each one a unique person.

It would be misleading to assume that all Frenchmen subscribed to the French school of thought. Alexis de Tocqueville evidenced deep roots in the English tradition of liberty. By the same token, many English intellectuals of the eighteenth and nineteenth centuries were entirely in the French rationalist camp: Priestley, Paine, and Bentham are clear cases in point. The great division between the two positions lay in their respective views of civilization. For the French school of liberty, civilization was raw material to be fashioned according to the philosopher's whims. For the English school of liberty, civilization was the accumulation of centuries of trial and error, a tender growth not to be discarded lightly for anyone's utopian plans.

Coleridge

Like many of the outstanding literary men of his generation, Samuel Taylor Coleridge at first had been strongly attracted to the French Revolution and its utopian goal of sweeping away all Man's corruption to replace it with the perfect society. The excesses of the Revolution soon brought a reaction. By 1798, Coleridge had discovered that the sweeping utopian vision of the perfect society led only to an even more bitter slavery than the French people had suffered before:

> When France in wrath her giant-limbs upreared, . . .
> Stamped her strong foot and said she would be free,
> Bear witness for me, how I hoped and feared! . . .
> The Sensual and the Dark rebel in vain,
> Slaves by their own compulsion! In mad game
> They burst their manacles and wear the name
> Of freedom, graven on a heavier chain!

Coleridge well understood that human happiness depended upon more than mere political forms. Instead, he emphasized inner, spiritual change, automatically suspecting the ruthless, secular, materialistic society that the rationalist planner was likely to create. He understood full well the necessity for inner growth of the individual as the only lasting means of social progress:

> One good consequence which I expect from [disillusionment with] revolution is that individuals will see, the necessity of individual effort; that they will act as good Christians, rather than as citizens and electors; and so by degrees will purge off . . . the error of atrributing to governments a talismanic influence over our virtues and our happiness, as if governments were not rather effects than causes.

Bentham

If Coleridge epitomized the English tradition of liberty, his fellow Englishman and contemporary Jeremy Bentham epitomized the French rationalist tradition. For Bentham, founder of Philosophic Radicalism, civilization was merely a large room filled with the furniture of social institutions, to be moved about and refashioned in whatever manner most likely to produce the ideal society. While it is true that Bentham attacked the ideology of the French Revolution, one wonders if he did not do so primarily because he distrusted the work of the French National Assembly, and would have preferred to have done the planning himself. There can be no doubt that Jeremy Bentham possessed a sentimental faith in human perfectibility, and in abstract rationalist philosophy to achieve that perfection. He reasoned to his conclusions about society from an *a priori* assumption, basing his celebrated calculus of pain and pleasure upon an abstract view of Man which saw no higher value in society than to maximize pleasure and minimize pain.

It is true that Bentham was a pronounced individualist in his economic philosophy, but his espousal of *laissez faire* was always based upon the grounds of utility. Thus, it was only a matter of time until the utilitarian position, with no underlying principle to guide it, would be led by its calculus of pleasure and pain toward egalitarian economics as a means of reducing pain and increasing pleasure. The connection between the utilitarianism of Jeremy Bentham and the Fabian socialism which came to dominate English society several generations later is far more immediate and direct than is generally recognized. Bentham and the Fabians were all too willing to regard men as little more than animals requiring a keeper. The great political struggle which took place in nineteenth-century England was essentially between the followers of the French rationalist tradition and the great Whig landowners. The Benthamites and the rest of the philosophic radicals triumphed in the end, and with that triumph expired the last best hope of saving liberalism from the clutches of rationalist, *a priori* reasoning.

It is true that Bentham and those who followed his line of thinking—most notably John Stuart Mill—were "libertarians" in the sense that they believed men to be more productive (and thus happier, in the pleasure-pain calculus) when society was free. But the *a priori* assumption at the root of their view of men envisioned a society sufficient unto itself, a society which could remake civilization and human nature as required, with no concern for a moral framework and no necessity for a faith in God. A system which thus leaves God out of its calculations tends to become dry-as-dust and in time opens the door to a new calculus—the horror of modern liberalism which willingly enslaves men in its quest to make them happy. Those "conservatives" who base their appeals exclusively on material progress, preaching endlessly about the number of refrigerators, automobiles, and flush toilets in our modern society, partake of the same error. The old pleasure-pain calculus thus rears its ugly head once again, obscuring and sometimes denying the infinitely more important moral point which underlies the case for freedom. In the process, it is small wonder that such crass materialism antagonizes many who would otherwise be attracted to the freedom ideal.

Mill

Readers of Mill's *On Liberty* may take issue with anyone attempting to characterize him as the connection between Jeremy Bentham and the Fabian Socialists. Surely the author of *On Liberty* must be a believer in human freedom. John Stuart Mill is an interesting case in point precisely because he could be simultaneously an apostle of individual freedom and a link in the process of degradation whereby liberalism became synonymous with socialism. He epitomizes better than any other thinker of his time the peculiar dichotomy destined to destroy the emphasis upon freedom within modern Liberalism.

The concluding words of *On Liberty* ring with libertarian spirit:

A state which dwarfs its men, in order that they may be more docile instruments in its hands even for beneficial purposes—will find that with small men no great thing can really be accomplished; and that the perfection of machinery to which it has sacrificed everything, will in the end avail it nothing, for want of the vital power which, in order that the machine might work smoothly, it has preferred to banish.

Mill had earlier examined the thought of Samuel Taylor Coleridge and Jeremy Bentham and had quite properly criticized Bentham for his belief that all human affairs could be reduced to a few tidy philosophic abstractions. Unfortunately, in his later work Mill fell into the same fatal trap. Under the influence of a woman whom he married late in life, Mill was led back to the same humanitarian abstractions which underlaid the Benthamite position. Before his death, he had become a socialist. He came to talk endlessly about "economic man," as though man could be separated by the rationalist into a series of component parts, to be analyzed, remodeled and reassembled according to "the greatest utility." Liberalism, divorced from its sound Whig roots in Adam Smith and Edmund Burke, was destined to slip into the same rationalist assumption that society could be remade according to abstract humanitarian principles. The rationalism of Bentham and Mill was destined to become the Fabianism of Shaw and the Webbs. If men would be free, they must base their freedom upon a faith in the individual and in civilization which is not so easily upset by utopian abstraction. Divorced from a theocentric view of human nature and civilization which insists upon an inviolable higher side to human personality, the merely utilitarian seems doomed to slide off into the corruptions of socialism.

Cobden

Richard Cobden was another of the key personalities who played a large role in transforming Whiggism into Liberalism. Cobden's thought centered exclusively around the idea of free trade. Although his Anti-Corn-Law League stressed the class conflict between the Whig landowners and the rising commercial interests, Cobden preferred to think of free trade as a law of nature, as a concept which society could reject only at its great peril. He saw the struggle against the great Whig landlords as a struggle against feudal limitations, as an attempt to substitute freedom and competition for all men in place of privilege and political intervention in favor of a few. He was so sure that free trade would solve all England's problems and thus benefit all Englishmen that he felt himself a defender of the old England, the England of the small landowner. Richard Cobden was trying to conserve traditional English society as he saw it, even though his principal opponents were the Whig landowners who had been the traditional defenders of English freedoms. Thus, in Cobden we see something of Burke's impulse to conserve, plus something of the rationalist enthusiasm for the perfect society.

This peculiar Cobden mixture of conservative and liberal, traditionalist and rationalist, was further compounded by a strong middle-class emphasis. Karl Marx was never more class-conscious than Richard Cobden. The group on which he pinned all his hopes for the salvation of society was the emerging middle class, the same group fated to give disastrous mismanagement to French political affairs between 1830 and 1848. Cobden totally rejected the Whig politics of the preceding 150 years, referring to it as "the worst thing that ever befell this country." He seemed to envision the perfect industrial society in which the industrious middle classes were destined to make modern England the envy of all the world.

In this way, Cobden was a utilitarian in the narrowest possible sense of the word. He tended to measure all social progress by middle-class material standards. In the process, the older Whig conservatism gave way to the newer style liberalism of Jeremy Bentham: "Make men prosperous and they will be happy." Cobden also epitomized the new liberalism in his emphasis upon John Stuart Mill's compartmentalization of man into his political and economic functions. As in Bentham and Mill and the rest of the nineteenth-century British liberals, Cobden's thought always tended to make too little of men by reducing them to such compartmentalized abstractions. This is harder to see in Cobden than in some of the other liberals, because he possessed certain homey intellectual vices which they did not, notably his preoccupation with the "solid and industrious middle class." In Cobden, as in the others of his generation, it is easy to find much with which we are sympathetic, but it is well to remind ourselves that their ideas contained the seeds from which modern democratic socialism would one day grow.

Cobbett

If the liberals of nineteenth-century England were beginning to show the shortcomings of their intellectual position, the conservatives were doing little better. The social questions involved in what shall be conserved and how it shall be conserved are among the most difficult in Christendom. The Whigs had conserved many of the institutions and traditions of individual freedom, but in the process they had also conserved their own privileges as feudal landowners. The attempted reforms of Bentham, Mill, and Cobden had been liberal in intent, yet had thrown out the baby with the bath and had paved the way for liberalism to become Fabian socialism. Meanwhile, some Englishmen were attempting to "conserve" portions of the English past which were already dead, and in the process were also helping to discredit freedom, albeit in their own special way. William Cobbett, the English journalist, politician and pamphleteer, is an obvious case in point. He was fond of talking about the simple, hearty life of the traditional English yeoman, centering on good drink, good food, and hard labor. For Cobbett, the nineteenth century was an uncomfortable time: everything was in a state of flux around him. He hated the machinery of the Industrial Revolution. He hated the idea of progress because it was breaking up the old fixed loyalties of England. Cobbett was so conservative that he became England's leading radical. He hated the new order so much that he was led to attack the important remaining portions of the old order. If Bentham and the utilitarians foresaw a materialist paradise on the road ahead, Cobbett was traveling the same road, though headed in the opposite direction. For that reason, Jeremy Bentham and William Cobbett, the would-be liberal and the would-be conservative, both looked to parliamentary reform and increasing political democracy as a means of achieving their diametrically opposed ends.

William Cobbett was a conservative of conservatives in his bitter opposition to the French Revolution and everything it stood for, yet so little understood its significance that he later came to view the Revolution as essentially beneficial, since it had destroyed Bourbon aristocracy, and "returned the French soil to the peasants." However incorrect and wrong-headed such wishful thinking might be concerning the actual events of the French Revolution, Cobbett was true to form in his response. He was never able to understand that "giving all political power to the people" might breed a new tyranny even more reprehensible than the old. For this reason, he led the way for political reform in England, playing a major role in the passage of the Reform Bill of 1832. Talking endlessly about the "rights of man" as a basis for his electoral reform, Cobbett never made the connection between such rationalist abstractions and the "Progress" to which he objected. He spoke with hatred of the materialist emphasis of the manufacturers coming to dominate England, and failed to realize that the whole basis of the political revolution he was helping to bring about hinged upon political exploitation of those same material appetites among the lower classes. Wishing to see the common people of England restored to the status of an earlier day ("I wish to see the poor men of England what the poor men of England were when I was born"), he believed that political means would conserve these values. Unfortunately for his peace of mind, he lived to see Parliament pass the new Poor Law, guaranteeing the final destruction of that hardy-yeoman independence of which he was so proud.

He was so desperately concerned with his misguided crusade that he finally came even to deny the property right, since some men had come to possess so much property that the balance of the older British society, which he presumably wished to conserve, had now been upset. For him the expropriation of property became a device by which traditional British society would be "conserved." He looked back with approval to the medieval prohibition of interest and loathed the whole financial system of credit and paper money. He hated the new order so bitterly that he was quite prepared to use massive political intervention to solve all problems. The result was not the conservation of Cobbett's beloved earlier English society, but the further destruction of British liberties which had centered on private property and the individual.

England Loses Her Way

By mid-century, English conservatives had forgotten what they were conserving. English liberals had forgotten what freedom meant, and the Whigs were dead beyond recall. The first fifty years of the nineteenth century had witnessed a steady decline in the institutions and ideas of freedom in England. As Hayek describes the change in *The Constitution of Liberty:*

> Bentham and his Utilitarians did much to destroy the beliefs which England had in part preserved from the Middle Ages by their scornful treatment of most of what until then had been the most admired features of the British constitution. And they introduced into Britain what had so far been entirely absent—the desire to remake the whole of her law and institutions on rational principles.

Perhaps we expect too much of Burke and the Whigs when we wonder why they were so unsuccessful in stemming the decline of individual freedom. Surely Burke faced formidable obstacles. He was confronted with an Industrial Revolution which carried with it the steadily rising material expectations of all classes. That these rising expectations should be vented through political channels, that political power could be used to plan the new technological utopia, seemed "self-evident" to several generations of Englishmen. We should not be surprised that English political life took such a direction. The Whigs suffered from another great disadvantage in their struggle for freedom: All political power was shifting from the Whig landowners to the new manufacturers, financiers, and merchants. The Industrial Revolution was generating its new ruling class.

Not surprisingly, the new ruling class brought with it middle-class democracy. The same currents which Bastiat so criticized in France between 1830 and 1848 were being felt in England as well. And, as Bastiat pointed out, if the political manipulation of human affairs is desirable for middle-class interests, why not political regulation of human affairs in the interests of the lower classes? Soon the contest for political power would dominate society.

The prophets of the new order must also bear a share of the blame. The open-ended society of Adam Smith, favoring freedom as primarily a *moral* goal, and viewing prosperity as an incidental accompanying blessing, gave way to a growing materialism in the thinking of the later Manchester School. In Ricardo and Malthus, it seems plain that the producer becomes subject to production, and men become subject to things. The "Iron Laws" of the new system not only whetted the appetite of the new industrial Europe, but also paved the way for reaction against the system. If the Iron Laws were indeed so immutable, then surely political power must be exercised to redress the balance. If the ultimate human values are material in nature, why not exercise political power to share this bounty? After Adam Smith, the substitution of the material for the moral robbed the Manchester School of its base of principle upon which a stand could be made.

Jeremy Bentham and his followers epitomized the new order. He reflected a political faith dominantly middle class and oriented to technology, the Industrial Revolution, and the development of what today would be called political administration. The Reform Act of 1832 was the first major step bringing about the desired political changes. Bougeois politics came into its own in the England of 1832 in a manner surprisingly similar to the Revolution of 1830 in France. Changes in both countries were equally revolutionary, with the only real difference centering around the characteristically English capacity for peaceful change and the seeming French necessity for violent change. The middle classes in both countries had high hopes: surely modern democratic politics had arrived, sweeping away privilege and replacing it with solid material values and technological "progress" for all. After 1832, the Chartist agitation began to bring pressure to bear for a further expansion of the franchise to include the English working classes. This was the tide which could no more be stopped in England than it had been in France. Once the old aristocracy and the bourgeoisie had begun to play class politics, one could rest assured that the working class would not long tolerate exclusion from the game. Marx was not far wrong in his assumption of class struggle; his only mistake was that he did not expect the struggle to be fought out for political benefits under a democratic regime.

As the nineteenth century reached its mid-point, it became clear that all shades of political opinion wished to play a role as the architects of a new England, with the remodeling process empowered by political pressures. People who called themselves "conservatives" wished to use political power to reverse the forces of change; people who called themselves "liberals" and "utilitarians" wished to use political power to speed the process of change. Those who recognized that the interventions of political power in the lives of men were likely to bring disaster in their wake were by now few in number, far from the seats of influence, and nameless, since all the labels had already been appropriated by those who were going to remodel England. The legislatures of such societies tend to resemble mad houses. When Ralph Waldo Emerson was visiting England, Thomas Carlyle showed him Parliament in session and asked bitterly, "Do you believe in the devil now?"

Of course, the new social radicalism of the middle classes did not proceed rapidly enough for those who urged total and immediate "reform." The new generation of politicians, sensing the direction of change, courted the favor of the aroused population, promising more and more in material benefits, and demanding less and less individual responsibility. Britain lagged only a few years behind France's timetable for the chaos which Bastiat fought in his last years. In Britain, the parties still took the names of Whig and Tory, but the new style Whigs and Tories were preaching the same doctrines to such an amazing extent that little real difference could be distinguished. The Whigs under Brougham had faint connection indeed with the party of Burke. The Tories under Disraeli gave much lip service to tradition, but carried through the most radical "social reforms" then known in nineteenth-century England. Surely the electoral reform of 1867, which took place under Tory direction, was the final blow to any limitation on the political process, much as the Revolutions of 1848 had been the final blow in France. No amount of Disraeli's rhetoric in praise of "tradition" can disguise that fact.

A few of the old-style friends of liberty remained on the scene, notably Sir Henry Maine, whose *Popular Government* was published in 1885. He applied the Burkean approach to the problems of nineteenth-century industrialism, and warned that liberty and equality were essentially incompatible. Liberty and civilization, both so deeply entangled with the concept of private property and individual rights, simply could not exist under a socialist tyranny, even though it chanced to be a "tyranny of the majority." Maine accurately predicted the course of modern democracy in virtually every country in the Western world when he wrote:

By a wise constitution, democracy may be made nearly as calm as
water in a great artificial reservoir; but if there is a weak point any-
where in the structure, the mighty forces which it controls will burst
through and spread destruction.

Well before the beginning of the twentieth century, the dam
had indeed burst in both England and France.

The American Whig

Burke, Tocqueville, Bastiat, and all the outstanding friends of
liberty in nineteenth-century Europe had always been quick to
notice one nation which seemed bent upon giving the fullest
possible development to the ideal of individual freedom and
private property. The United States of America seemed to be
the one outstanding example of how such a system might operate in practice. Indeed, the American Revolution had come
about primarily because Britain had insisted upon interfering
with the political and economic freedom of the thirteen colonies. Burke and the Whigs of his time had warmly supported
the American colonists against the British crown. At the same
time, the colonists had warmly supported the English Whigs,
since they perceived that most of the guiding principles of the
new republic had their origins deep in established Whig principles of limited government and the rule of law.

Unfortunately, the American use of the political term
"Whig" as it developed in the nineteenth century degenerated
into a label for a party of political hacks, much as the name had
degenerated in England. Despite the corruption of the name,
Whig principles lived on for much of nineteenth-century
American history. Often the student of American history is
asked to choose between the alleged radicalism of Jefferson and

the alleged conservatism of Hamilton, but the guiding spirit of the nineteenth century at its best is more properly centered in the ideas of James Madison, America's nearest approach to the traditional Whig statesman. The ideal of limited government and economic free enterprise, allowing the free play of interests in the market place, had already been foreshadowed in the colonial experience and became the working definition of society in nineteenth-century America. It was because the old Whig tradition was so deeply rooted in American society that the corruptions of modern industrial democracy took longer to erode the system, though today we are awash in the same sea of unprincipled confusion which earlier swept France and England.

France

If Frederic Bastiat had few allies abroad, he had even fewer at home. In a world gone mad with the egalitarian, materialistic politics of the age, one of those French allies was the distinguished historian Hippolyte Taine. In his scholarship, Taine played the same role as Sir Henry Maine did in England. Besieged from all sides, Taine insisted that French centralization was smothering individual freedom. He criticized the urban regime, but insisted that the French republicans and liberals were going even farther toward freedom-destroying centralization than the Bourbons had ever contemplated. Strongly conservative, Taine valued the traditional decentralization of an earlier day, and described the sound independence and individual variation which decentralization could once again bring to France if all the slogans and grand abstractions of centralization were brought to an end once and for all.

Tocqueville

More than any other contemporary of Bastiat, Alexis de Tocqueville shared Bastiat's bitter opposition to the centralizing tendencies of French society. Since Tocqueville was more likely to stress tradition and established historical forms of freedom, while Bastiat was more likely to emphasize freedom as an abstraction, or as a "law of nature," the temptation comes immediately to mind to compare Tocqueville as the conservative and Bastiat as the libertarian. Actually, as we shall see, there was much of the conservative in Bastiat, much of the libertarian in Tocqueville. Neither Bastiat nor Tocqueville would have hesitated to identify the enemy as the centralizing power of big government. It is highly unlikely that they would have allowed any mere difference in labels to cause them to turn upon one another while forgetting the identity of the real enemy.

The parallels between the two men are numerous. Not only did their life spans closely coincide, but they spent the majority of their lives in quiet study and retirement from the world. Both Bastiat and Tocqueville had a brief fling at public life in the turbulence of mid-nineteenth-century French politics.

Best known for his famous *Democracy in America,* Tocqueville was quick to praise the equality of opportunity which accompanied American democracy, but predicted with penetrating accuracy the ways in which American democracy might finally lose all freedom in its pursuit of an ephemeral equality.

The young French aristocrat brought the same penetrating insight to his analysis of French politics. He consistently opposed the older evils of the French monarchy and the newer evils of the French democracy, realizing that political power was likely to be abused by anyone who held too much of it. Like Bastiat, he lacked the qualities which marked the practical politican, and had his primary impact in his writing.

Tocqueville's genius lay in the broad historical perspective which he brought to his analysis. For example, he recognized that the Revolution of 1848 was not the end but the beginning of a new phase in French politics. Like Marx, Tocqueville recognized the fact that the great struggle of the times was destined to be a class struggle over property:

> The time will come when the country will find itself once again divided between two great parties. The French Revolution which abolished all privileges and destroyed all exclusive rights, has allowed one to remain, that of property. Let not the proprietors deceive themselves as to the strength of their position, nor think that the rights of property form an insurmountable barrier because they have not as yet been surmounted; for our times are unlike any others. When the rights of property were merely the origin and commencement of a number of other rights, they were easily defended, or rather, they were never attacked; they then formed the surrounding wall of society, of which all other rights were the outposts; no blows reached them; no serious attempt was ever made to touch them. But to-day, when the rights of property are nothing more than the last remnants of an overthrown aristocratic world; when they alone are left intact, isolated privileges amid the universal levelling of society; when they are no longer protected behind a number of still more controvertible and odious rights, the case is altered, and they alone are left daily to resist the direct and unceasing shock of democratic opinion. . . .

> Before long, the political struggle will be restricted to those who have and those who have not; property will form the great field of battle; and the principal political questions will turn upon the more or less important modifications to be introduced into the right of property. We shall then have once more among us great public agitations and great political parties.

Tocqueville regarded property as the foundation of the social order, the right which could not be abridged without destroying all liberty, and, as a final result, all civilization. He warned that the centralization of society, which would be carried even farther under the new republic than it had been under the old monarchy, would bring with it an instability and an unrest likely to destroy all freedoms. For Tocqueville, a society not founded upon habit, tradition, and custom was likely to be a society not of reform, but disaster.

He especially concerned himself with the absence of an aristocracy of talent capable of directing the new democratic currents. Tocqueville recognized that democracy was clearly the inevitable tendency of the nineteenth and twentieth centuries, but he feared that the zest for a literal equality of condition would sweep away all guarantees of individual personality, once the barriers of custom and tradition had been removed. He expected that the discrepancy between political equality and economic inequality would pave the way for demagogues to gain political power on the strength of their promises to equalize economic conditions.

Tocqueville feared that the resultant sweep of liberty, equality, and fraternity would in practice only give a pseudo-religious quality to a crusade of envy and hatred. He saw the repeated French revolutions of the late eighteenth and mid-nineteenth centuries as the result of what hc called "absolute systems." The totally abstract philosophies of the eighteenth and nineteenth-century rationalists, promising the blueprint of a perfect society, of a heaven on earth, seemed to Tocqueville to be the real source of the constant revolutions and repressions stemming from the new democratic order. He belived that the *a priori* blueprints of the perfect society, the endless discussion of "rights" derived not from concrete historical experience but from abstract appeals to nature, were calculated to lead society ever further astray. He warned that human history gave no evidence of a potential perfection present in human nature, and pointed out that Man proved to be a convenient abstraction whereby some men forced their ideas on others. Protesting against the "tyranny of the majority" and against projections of the perfect society as hatched in the brain of some philosopher, Tocqueville insisted upon the necessity of traditional standards and institutions as the only means of preserving liberty. Thus, on most counts, Alexis de Tocqueville was a Burkean conservative. Like Burke, he was willing to accept change and modification of society, provided the change was not revolutionary and utopian in nature. Tocqueville could accept the new age of democracy, if democracy meant an equality of opportunity and the liberty for each man fully to develop his own talents. But he warned that a society cut loose from its moorings would be likely to introduce not an equality of opportunity, but an equality of condition, with all of the terrible repressions which accompany such a political scheme. The events of the nineteenth century proved him entirely correct.

What's In a Name?

In the preceding discussion of some of the political and intellectual leaders commonly associated with the England and France of Bastiat's day, considerable confusions are likely to enter the scene. The words "conservative," "liberal," "Whig," "libertarian" make their appearance as labels of various men and various ideas. At times all share a common opposition to big government; at other times all have been corrupted into a variety of bizarre meanings.

It is well to bear in mind that "Conservative" means many

things, depending upon what we are conserving and how we are doing it. Unfortunately, not all conservatives are of the stature of a Burke or a Tocqueville.

By the same token, "liberal" has been so completely divorced from its original connotation of "favoring least government" that it can now be accurately characterized as "favoring most government." That corruption came about because the liberal position has tended to be abstract in nature and has tended to regard human perfectibility as an *a priori* condition. As the rsult, *Man* has often been substituted for God. Inevitably in such ideas, the concept soon makes its appearance that Man, since he is master of his own destiny, can better manipulate society to his own advantage. We live in an age which clearly reflects the results of such thinking.

"Libertarian" is a coined word, taken up by the advocates of freedom when the word liberal was rendered totally unusable. But it is worth recollection that the word libertarian stems from the same philosophic roots as "liberal" and thus can potentially suffer from the same corruptions. If we turn our back on all past historic tradition, and on the idea of a Superior Power which presides over the universe, we are likely to find ourselves trapped in a philosophic position in which no defenses remain against the super state. A potentially equal danger is the possibility of over-reaction against government. If not restrained, such a reaction can produce a craving for philosophic anarchy. At that point, property and the other institutions guaranteeing individual liberty will cease to exist as surely as if they were destroyed by the omnipotent state.

Perhaps the potential corruptions of these terms explain the reason why Friedrich Hayek prefers to call himself a Whig. But no one knows better than Professor Hayek that the Whig position has also been subject to its corruptions. It seems that politics will distort practically any philosophic position or label.

Yet, conservative, liberal, libertarian and Whig, at their best, all stand as a portion of the antidote for the statist poison of our times. It is true that the politics and ideas of the late eighteenth and early nineteenth centuries leave a tangled trail for those advocates of liberty who are seeking a philosophic position and a defensible name. Perhaps Frederic Bastiat's most lasting significance will prove to lie in the fact that he offers some solutions to our problem. He lived through the complexities of the age, and was subjected to the currents and cross-currents of thought which we have just discussed. A careful analysis of Bastiat's place in this complex picture offers insights of real value in our search for firm ground in an age whose confusions are even more aggravated than were the confusions of Bastiat's day.

Bastiat and His Place in the Scheme of Things

Frederic Bastiat was no admirer of the past. In this sense, he was far closer to French radicalism than English conservatism. One of his rare references to Alexis de Tocqueville criticized Tocqueville's defense of primogentiure and aristocratic privilege as socially useful devices. Bastiat was quick to undercut what he regarded as the hero worship of the past:

> Distance contributes not a little to give to ancient figures a quality of grandeur. If someone speaks to us of the Roman citizen, we ordinarily do not picture to ourselves a brigand occupied with acquiring booty and slaves, at the expense of peaceful peoples; we do not see him half-naked, shockingly dirty, going about muddy streets; we do not surprise him in the act of flogging a slave until the blood flows or putting him to death if he shows a bit of energy and spirit. We prefer to picture to ourselves a beautiful head crowning an impressive and

majestic body draped like an ancient statue. We like to think of him
as meditating on the high destinies of his country. He seems to us to
be seeing his family gathering around the hearth, which is honored
by the presence of the gods; the wife preparing the simple repast of
the warrior and glancing with confidence and admiration at her husband's face; the young children attentive to the discourse of an old
man who whiles away the hours by recounting the exploits and the
virtues of their father. . . .

Oh, what illusions would be dissipated if we could evoke the past,
walk down the streets of Rome, and see close up the men whom, from
afar, we admire so naively! . . .

On repeated occasions, he insisted that the social and moral
triumphs of human behavior lay not in the past, but the future.
For him the idea of perfection belonged not at the beginning
of time, but at the end. Thus he was quick to criticize the
conservative emphasis upon tradition, habit, and custom.

Democracy

His faith in the future caused him largely to accept the democratic assumptions of his age. Bastiat seemed to feel that, unless
one believed in the capacity of men to solve problems and to
advance civilization, we were doomed to return to the anti-
democratic repressions of the past. However, like Tocqueville,
Bastiat was quick to point out that, despite his democratic
sympathies, he was strongly opposed to those who proclaimed
themselves the exclusive representatives of democracy:

Whatever the disciples of Rousseau's school, who call themselves *very
much advanced,* and whom I believe to be twenty centuries *behind
the times,* may think of it, universal suffrage (taking this word in its
strict sense) is not one of those sacred dogmas which it is a crime to
examine or doubt.

He emphasized that the distortions of democracy, as practiced by the social architects, was little more than a mere use
of the people to gain political power. In making this point,
Bastiat drew on the ample evidence present in the French
politics of his own time. The democracy, or "rule of the people," which Bastiat did favor stemmed from a completely different premise than Rousseau's *General Will* and the mass
actions likely to stem from it. For Bastiat, the rule of the people
could be best achieved in a system which allowed the individuals of society to go their own way without placing restraints
upon them:

> You contend that I am wrong to practice Catholicism; and I contend
> that you are wrong to practice Lutheranism. Let us leave it to God
> to judge. Why should I strike at you, or why should you strike at me?
> If it is not good that one of us should strike at the other, how can it
> be good that we should delegate to a third party, who controls the
> public police force, the authority to strike at one of us in order to
> please the other?

> You contend that I am wrong to teach my son science and philosophy;
> I believe you are wrong to teach yours Greek and Latin. Let us both
> follow the dictates of our conscience. Let us allow the law of responsi-
> bility to operate for our families. It will punish the one who is wrong.
> Let us not call in human law; it could well punish the one who is not
> wrong.

Bastiat felt that public opinion should be sovereign, but that
it should also be enlightened. He fully appreciated that the only
lasting enlightenment of public opinion was a direct cause-and-
effect relationship with experience. Make people responsible
for their own actions and all the consequences thereof, and
public enlightenment will soon be achieved. He warned that the
people would always have corruptors on hand to attempt lead-

ing them astray, and insisted that no amount of rhetoric could possibly hope to stem that corruption until individual responsibility became the order of society. The great task for those who wished to give lasting improvement to the world around them was to divorce themselves completely from the problem-solving of politics, substituting the really effective solution for all problems, enlightenment of the *individuals* composing society. Bastiat's faith in the people was not founded upon the people *en masse* or upon any other democratic slogans. He recognized that the only action of lasting value, for the individual or for his society, was not political action, but personal action.

The Nature of Man

Unlike John Stuart Mill and the utilitarians who had preceded him, Bastiat did not make the mistake of dividing man into abstract and unreal segments such as "political man" or "economic man." He was quite prepared to insist that religious sentiment, loyalty, love, friendship, patriotism, charity, and the whole spectrum of human social and moral values were inseparable from man's economic life. Bastiat insisted upon a higher side to human nature, and a meaning of ultimate value to all human transactions. He derived this higher side from a simple premise:

> In this book there is a central, dominant thought; it pervades every page, it gives life and meaning to every line. It is the thought that begins the Christian's creed: *I believe in God.*

Building upon that belief in a Superior Power, Bastiat made it abundantly clear that he did not believe in the perfectibility of human nature or in the achievement of any utopian heaven on earth:

Evil exists. It is inherent in human frailty; it evidences itself in the moral order as in the physical order, in the mass as in the individual, in the whole as in its parts. Because our eyes may hurt and our sight grow dim, will the physiologist ignore the harmonious mechanism of these wonderful organs? Will he deny the ingenious structure of the human body because that body is subject to pain, illness and death, because Job once cried out in his despair: "I have said to corruption, Thou art my father, to the worm, Thou art my mother and my sister!" In the same manner, because the social order will never bring mankind safely to port in the fantastic dreamland of absolute good, must the economist refuse to recognize the marvelous structure of the social order, which is so constituted as to diffuse more and more enlightenment, morality, and happiness among more and more people?

Thus, even though man is not perfectible, he does have a higher side, an understanding of the good and the right which may be cultivated. In that cultivation, the individual and his society may progress. Bastiat stands with Burke, not only on the grounds that human nature is not perfectible and that utopias are not possible of fulfillment, but also on the grounds that men have both the obligation and the opportunity to improve themselves, and, in so doing, improve their society.

In Bastiat's view of the nature of man, we find the same emphasis upon *responsibility* which he so often insisted upon in his discussions of democracy and a proper social order:

Genesis relates how, when the first man had been driven from the earthly paradise because he had learned to distinguish right from wrong—*to know good and evil*—God pronounced this sentence upon him: *In sorrow shalt thou eat of it* [*the fruit of the earth*] *all the days of thy life. Thorns and thistles shall it bring forth to thee. . . . In the sweat of thy face shalt thou eat bread, till thou return unto the ground, for out of it wast thou taken; for dust thou art and unto dust shalt thou return.*

Here, then, we have good and evil—or human nature. Here we have acts and habits producing good or bad consequences—or human nature. Here are toil, sweat, thorns, tribulation, and death—or human nature.

Human nature, I say: for to choose, to err, to suffer, to correct one's errors—in a word, all the elements that make up the idea of responsibility—are so much a part of our sentient, intelligent, and free nature, they are so much one with this nature, that I defy the most fertile imagination to conceive of any other kind of existence for man.

His opposition to the social architects stemmed in large part from his insistence upon this idea of responsibility. Warning that effort and satisfaction are indissolubly joined, he decried the attempts of nineteenth-century society to separate the two and to attempt the creation of a perverted social order which pretended that men need not be responsible for their acts:

Political economy has not been given the mission of finding out what society would be like if it had pleased God to make man different from what he is. It may be regrettable that Providence, at the beginning, neglected to seek the advice of some of our modern social reformers ... if He had not disregarded the advice of Fourier, the social order would have borne no resemblance to the one in which we are obliged to live, breathe, and move about. But, since we are in it, since we do live, move, and have our being in it, our only recourse is to study it and to understand its laws, especially if the improvement of our condition essentially depends upon such knowledge.

Those laws of human nature which Bastiat felt men must come to study and understand were simply that human life demanded of us foresight, labor, virtue, and the exercise of will, since to be human was to rise above man's finite nature and to develop those traits of character and personality whereby we could occupy the place intended for us in God's scheme of things on earth. He warned that any other course would lead downward, to a degradation of both the individual and his society.

The Nature of Government

We hold from God the gift that for us includes all other gifts: life—physical, intellectual, and moral life.

But life is not self-sustaining. He who gave it to us has left to us the responsibility of preserving it, of developing it, of perfecting it . . .

Each of us certainly gets from Nature, from God, the right to defend his person, his liberty, and his property, since they are the three elements constituting or sustaining life, elements which are mutually complementary and which cannot be understood without one another. For what are our faculties, if not an extension of our personality, and what is property, if not an extension of our faculties?

If each man has the right to defend, even by force, his person, his liberty, and his property, several men have the right to get together, come to an understanding, and organize a collective force to provide regularly for this defense.

Collective right, then, has its principle, its *raison d'etre,* its legitimate basis, in individual right; and the collective force can rationally have no other end, no other function, than that of the individual forces for which it substitutes.

Thus Bastiat insisted that collective force could only be used to insure the life, liberty, and property of individuals. While his position severely limited the role of government, Bastiat was far from adopting a position of philosophic anarchy. He went on to point out that man is primarily a social creature in nature, since:

> The members of society have certain needs that are so general, so
> universal, that provision is made for them by organizing *government
> services.* Among these requirements is the need for security. People
> agree to tax themselves in order to pay, in the form of *services* of
> various kinds, those who perform the service of seeing to the common
> security.

The philosophic anarchists of Bastiat's time and our own
have been quick to insist that, if all rights derive from the
individual, then no constraints of police power and no taxation
may properly be levied by any collective force on the individual. Of course, both the philosophic anarchist at one pole and
the advocate of all powerful government at the other pole share
the rationalist assumption that human nature is perfectible,
thus paving the way for a faith in Man to replace a faith in God.
It would be well if all men behaved in such a manner requiring
no government protection of life, liberty, and property, just as
it would be well if big government could really further the
well-being of the individuals composing society. Unfortunately, a flawed human nature makes both of these extremes
impossible.

Bastiat's insistence upon the presence of evil in the world,
and his firm faith in God, ruled out the possibility of both
philosophic anarchy and big government as proper organizational principles for the formation of society. If the concept of
individual rights derives from a faith in God, then the recognition of a spiritual dignity within each of us serves as a bulwark
against anyone who would manipulate society. But if God is
replaced by Man, a perfectible and self-sufficient being, the
basis for individual rights is removed. Heaven on earth
becomes a tangible goal, and the systems-builders are freed
from all restraints. Some would make the government the be-
all and end-all of society; others would deny all place for gov-

ernment, presumably leaving our lives and property to the tender mercies of "perfectible Man." Such people mistakenly class themselves as libertarians, forgetting that a man not safe in his life and property is far from free. For Bastiat, government had to be given a monopoly of force, insuring that no individual in society could exercise force or fraud against any other. Of course, Bastiat also insisted that this governmental monopoly of force could only be negative in character, and must have no use except for the *prevention* of force and fraud:

> Hence, if anything is self-evident, it is this: Law is the organization of the natural right to legitimate self-defense; it is the substitution of collective force for individual forces, to act in the sphere in which they have the right to act, to do what they have the right to do: to guarantee security of person, liberty, and property rights, to cause *justice* to reign over all.

> And if there existed a nation constituted on this basis, it seems to me that order would prevail there in fact as well as in theory. It seems to me that this nation would have the simplest, most economical, least burdensome, least disturbing, least officious, most just, and consequently most stable government that can be imagined, whatever its political form might be.

Insisting that "law is justice," Bastiat warned that any attempt to use the law to oppress man's person or plunder his property, even for a philanthropic end, was to destroy the basis of justice upon which the whole system depended.

The Nature of Society

One of the areas where Bastiat is most strongly in the French rationalist tradition is in the position he implicitly adopts concerning the nature of society. Bastiat takes the rationalist position when he argues for a society based upon abstract principle, rather than discussing society as an organic growth, as did Tocqueville and Burke. Society is *sui generis*. It is impossible to conceive of a time when no social order existed; men have always lived in a society of one sort or another. Of course, to base one's views of the social order on an abstract and imaginary moment in man's existence before the creation of society is clearly in the French rationalist tradition. Bastiat thus was combatting the dominant ideas of the French Revolution in the France of his day, but he himself sometimes used the same tools of rationalist abstraction as did those whom he fought.

Where Tocqueville would be concrete and historical, Bastiat would sometimes be rationalist. For example, if Tocqueville would say, "John Smith has a right to defend his life," Bastiat was sometimes prone to say, "Man has a right to defend his property." If Tocqueville would insist that "government has always existed in some form or another," Bastiat would at times seem to assume, without actually saying so, "Man originally lived in a state of nature and has only lately established government by contract." It is of course from this second position, the rationalist position, that most of the serious errors of our time, both of the no-government and the super-government variety have derived. Basing his case upon rationalist abstraction, Bastiat thus flirts with error on two counts: in his idea of his collective "We"; and in his idea that there is a contractual basis to society.

The collective "We" will not bear close examination, since there is absolutely nothing about a series of individual rights which produces a collective right. To discuss the rights which the individual derives from the Creator as though they were equivalent with the Rights of Man moves us from the sanity of Burke to the insanity of the French Revolution. Bastiat's

second implicit error, his assumption that society has a contractual basis, partakes of the same departure from concrete
human experience. It is here that Bastiat is least conservative
and most rationalist. Still, Bastiat escaped the rationalist trap
in his own thinking because he avoided the confusion between
"progress" and "perfectibility" which plagues most of the
thinkers who have relied upon abstractions.

Frederic Bastiat had a faith in the capacity of men to achieve
progress. But he did not believe that human nature was perfect
or perfectible:

> . . . all the . . . great objectives that mankind pursue . . . are all
> constantly approached, but never perfectly attained.

He knew that, "an absolute degree of any good thing whatsoever would mean the extinction of all desire, all effort, all
planning, all thought, all foresight, all virtue; perfection ex-
cludes perfectibility." Basing his view upon the existence of a
God who had created the individual in all his spiritual dignity,
Bastiat urged the possibility of progress. Men must be imperfect, or they would already be gods; and yet men must be
capable of improvement, unless we are to deny the existence of
a higher striving in man.

Building upon this idea, Bastiat insisted that man was by
nature a social being, since, without cooperation, there could
be no society, and without society and its resultant cooperation, man would have no opportunity to progress, to fulfill his
higher destiny and thereby give purpose to his existence. Thus
social order, like freedom, was a prerequisite for men to allow
them their fullest scope of operation. The social order was
therefore a law of Providence, a necessary precondition for

mankind moving upward from the low level of perfection then evident in the world.

The adoption of such a position leaves Bastiat poles apart from those who see human nature as perfect or perfectible:

> If man were perfect, if he were infallible, society would present a very different kind of harmony from that which we may actually expect it to offer us. Our idea of harmony is not Fourier's. It does not exclude the existence of evil; it leaves room for discord; and yet we shall recognize that harmony nonetheless exists, provided that discord serves to prepare the way and to lead us back to harmony.

> This is our starting point: man is fallible, and God has given him free will and, with his ability to choose, also the ability to err, to mistake the false for the true, to sacrifice the future for the present, to yield to the unreasonable desires of his own heart.

> Man makes mistakes. But every act and habit has its consequences.

Thus Bastiat returned to the necessity for limited government, neither too great nor too little to protect the social order and allow the harmonious development of society, a development premised upon the individual's full responsibility for his own shortcomings. Society would progress to the extent that it allowed individuals to be fully and truly themselves:

> "Know thyself"—is, as the oracle says, the beginning, the middle, and the end of the moral and political sciences.

> We have stated elsewhere that, in regard to man or human society, harmony cannot mean perfection, but progress toward perfection. Now, progress toward perfection always implies some degree of imperfection in the future as well as in the past. If man could ever enter the promised land of *absolute good,* he would have no further need of his intelligence or of his senses; he would no longer be man.

Frederic Bastiat understood what so many abstract thinkers have forgotten. To be fully and truly themselves, men must be allowed to act as men, neither reduced to automatons, nor raised to the level of gods.

Inequality and Injustice

If men were to be treated as men, neither more nor less, then the fact of pain and hardship had to be accepted as a reality which had always been part of the human condition. As Bastiat viewed the history of man, he found himself convinced that sin and suffering had always been man's lot:

> It can well be maintained that it was inevitable that injustice should come into the world, that society could not have escaped it; and, granted man's nature, with his passions, his selfishness, his original ignorance and improvidence, I believe it.

Far from finding the suffering of man as a limiting factor, Bastiat viewed the limitless number of unfulfilled human wants as the strongest possible incentive for exercise of our faculties in the attempted fulfillment of those wants. As he phrased it, "Man wants to improve his lot. This is the first law of his nature."

There are only two ways in which each of us can improve our lot: at our own expense; or at the expense of others. The first method constitutes justice; the second, injustice. While we all oppose injustice in the abstract, how many men follow Bastiat's advice?

> He should perhaps ask himself whether the cause of such social conditions is not ancient acts of plunder, effected by way of conquest, and more recent acts of plunder, effected by the intervention of the

law. He should ask himself whether, granted the aspiration of all men
towards well-being and self-fulfillment, the reign of justice would not
be enough to set the forces of progress into rapid motion and to realize
the greatest amount of equality compatible with that individual responsibility which God has ordained as the just retribution for virtue
and vice.

In short, we all hate injustice and inequality, but more of us
should understand that often injustice and inequality are the
direct results of using the force of the law to favor some at the
expense of others.

If men are to work with their limited capacities to satisfy
their unlimited wants, society can progress so long as the individuals involved are left free to progress and to compete one
with another in satisfying their own wants to the extent that
they satisfy the wants of others. Unfortunately, this competi-
tive ideal often is not given a chance to work in modern society:

> . . . competition in modern society is far from playing its natural role.
> Our laws inhibit it at least as much as they encourage it; and to answer
> the question whether inequality is due to the presence or the absence
> of competition, we need only observe who the men are who occupy
> the limelight and dazzle us with their scandalous fortunes, to assure
> ourselves that inequality, in so far as it is artificial and unjust, is based
> on conquest, monopolies, restrictions, privileged positions, high gov-
> ernment posts and influence, administrative deals, loans from the
> public funds—with all of which competition has no connection.

One of the direct results of the injustices stemming from the
special privileges is that the inequalities and sufferings within
society are bound to grow steadily worse. The more government intervenes, the more severe the distresses are likely to be.
Soon the suffering and resentment is so keen that the people
come to believe that the existing political regime must be re-

placed. In Bastiat's time, four such revolutionary changes had taken place, yet each change seemed to leave the French people worse off than before. Bastiat knew why political change always seemed to be for the worse, anticipating a fact of political science that is now widely recognized:

> Once an abuse exists, everything is arranged on the assumption that it will last indefinitely; and, as more and more people come to depend upon it for their livelihood, and still others depend upon them, a superstructure is erected that soon comprises a formidable edifice.

> The moment you try to tear it down, everybody protests; and the point to which I wish to call particular attention here is that those who protest always appear at first glance to be in the right, because it is easier to show the disorder that must accompany reform than the order that should follow it.

Bastiat invariably looked to the United States as the model of a free society. Yet even here he perceived that injustice existed, injustice likely to produce the greatest suffering:

> Is there any need to prove that this odious perversion of the law is a perpetual cause of hatred, discord, and even social disorder? Look at the United States. There is no country in the world where the law confines itself more rigorously to its proper role, which is to guarantee everyone's liberty and property. Accordingly, there is no country in which the social order seems to rest on a more stable foundation. Nevertheless, even in the United States there are two questions, and only two, which since it was founded, have several times put the political order in danger. And what are these two questions? The question of slavery and that of tariffs, that is, precisely the only two questions concerning which, contrary to the general spirit of this republic, the law has assumed a spoliative character. Slavery is a violation, sanctioned by law, of the rights of the person. Protective tariffs are a violation, perpetrated by the law, of the right to property; and certainly it is remarkable that in the midst of so many other disputes this twofold *legal scourge,* a sad heritage from the Old

World, should be the only one that can and perhaps will lead to the dissolution of the Union. It is, in fact, impossible to imagine any graver situation in a society than one in which the law becomes an instrument of injustice. And if this fact gives rise to such dreadful consequences in the United States, where it is only exceptional, what must be its consequences in Europe, where it is a principle and a system?

Progress and Harmony

If inequality and injustice are the inevitable concomitants of political interventions in the lives of men beyond the protection of life, liberty, and property, what are the conditions necessary for progress and harmony for the human spirit? Bastiat felt that redemption did exist for both the individual and for the human race. For the individual, redemption lies in the proper ordering of one's immortal soul. For the human race, it lies in proper ordering of the social system which would allow for the progress and harmony of all men within the social order. For Bastiat, as in so many other elements of his thinking, the key to that harmonious and progressive social order was the self-responsible individual:

> This is how they understand freedom and democracy in the United States. There each citizen is vigilant with a jealous care to remain his own master. It is by virtue of such freedom that the poor hope to emerge from poverty, and that the rich hope to preserve their wealth.

> And, in fact, as we see, in a very short time this system has brought the Americans to a degree of enterprise, security, wealth, and equality of which the annals of the human race offer no other example.

Since self-preservation and self-development are conditions to which all men naturally aspire, the greater the freedom allowed men in the exercise of their faculties, the greater the progress of society as a whole. In a society in which injustice is prohibited by government, the very fact of self-preservation and self-development as a basic condition of human nature would insure that, as the individual would do for himself, he would also do for society.

At times, Bastiat leaned rather toward the rationalist French tradition in his treatment of the subject of progress. He believed that progress was the destiny of the human race and saw the road to that progress through self-responsibility, which would offer the necessary experience for the individual to learn from his mistakes. In his simultaneous emphasis upon learning from experience and using that experience to progress into the future, thus looking both backward and forward in human experience, Bastiat stood at some mid-point between the rationalist and the conservative:

> From earliest childhood to extreme old age, life is a long apprenticeship. We learn to walk by repeated falls; we learn by hard and repeated experiences to avoid heat, cold, hunger, thirst, excesses. We complain that experience is a hard teacher; but if it were not, we should never learn anything.
>
> The same is true of the moral order. The awful consequences of cruelty, injustice, terror, violence, fraud, and idleness, are what teach us to be kind, just, brave, temperate, honest, and industrious. Experience takes a long time; it will, indeed, always be at work but it is effective.
>
> Since such is man's nature, it is impossible not to recognize in responsibility the mainspring of social progress. It is the crucible of experience.

Bastiat never tired of pointing out that the total number of satisfactions for any member of society is always far greater than the number he could secure by his own efforts. He insisted that there was an obvious disproportion between a man's consumption and his labor. This improvement of the condition of the individual was brought about by social cooperation, by the development of a God-given pattern of progress which carried everyone along with it to progressively greater heights unless political intervention entered the scene. He did not feel that the exercise of free will limited society. Indeed, he felt it was the exercise of free will which made society possible:

> . . . because I believe that a higher Power directs it, because, since God can intervene in the moral order only through the instrumentality of each man's self-interst and will, the resulting action of various interests and wills cannot lead to ultimate evil; for otherwise it would not be man or the human race alone that is on the road to error, but God Himself who, in virtue of His impotence or cruelty, would be leading His imperfect creature on to evil.

> We therefore believe in liberty because we believe in the harmony of the universe, that is, in God. Proclaiming in the name of faith, formulating in the name of science, the divine laws, flexible and vital, of our dynamic moral order, we utterly reject the narrow, unwieldy, and static institutions that some men in their blindness would heedlessly introduce into this admirable mechanism. It would be absurd for an atheist to say: *Laissez faire!* Leave it to chance! But we, who are believers, have the right to cry: *Laissez passer!* Let God's order and justice prevail! Let human initiative, the marvelous and unfailing transmitter of all man's motive power, function freely! And freedom, thus understood, is no longer an anarchistic deification of individualism; what we worship, above and beyond man's activity, is God directing all.

Reasoning from such a premise, Bastiat was anxious to refute the gloomy theories of Ricardo and Malthus, to point out that the harmonious working of the laws of nature would produce results beneficial to mankind. Thus Bastiat found the teachings of the Manchester School too narrow. The endless talk about "Iron Laws" which would limit all men to a subsistence wage simply did not jibe with the expansive view of men and society which Bastiat possessed. The development of the modern industrial order since Bastiat's time has supported his position, since most workers have progressed far beyond subsistence wages, producing in the Western world the first predominantly middle-class society, in whose material prosperity almost all members of society have participated.

The point at which Bastiat went beyond the rationalist ideas of the Physiocrats, and the earlier free market economists, was his recognition of the fact that no fundamental incompatibility existed between the welfare of one man and the welfare of all. He recognized that the incompatibilities had been introduced into society by those who had attempted to manipulate society politically for the advantage of some group at the expense of others. Bastiat based this idea primarily upon a fundamental faith in God: "*. . . what God does, He does well. . . .*" In his religious faith, and in the distinction which Bastiat made between perfection and progress, Bastiat clearly rejects the customary rationalist position. He reveals himself almost a Burkean conservative. We must say "almost" because he also projected a very un-Burkean enthusiasm for a future which would dwarf the past:

> Thus, I repeat, . . . harmony does not mean the idea of absolute perfection, but the idea of unlimited progress. It has pleased God to attach suffering to our nature, since He has willed that we move from weakness to strength, from ignorance to knowledge, from want to satisfaction, from effort to result, from acquisition to possession, from privation to wealth, from error to truth, from experience to foresight. I bow without murmur before this decree, for I cannot imagine how else our lives could have been ordered. If, then, by means of a mech-

anism as simple as it is ingenious, He has arranged that *all men should be brought closer together on the way toward a constantly rising standard of living,* if He thus guarantees them—through the very action of what we call evil—lasting and more widely distributed progress, then, not content with bowing before this generous and powerful hand, I bless it, I marvel at it, and I adore it.

Self-interest

How would this harmony and progress be achieved? What would be the qualities of a society in which men were left free to make their own choices? Bastiat felt that the motive forces in the free society would be self-interest and property:

> Man is cast upon this earth. He is irresistibly drawn toward happiness and repelled by suffering. Since his actions are determined by these impulses, it cannot be denied that self-interest is his great motive force as an individual, as it is of all individuals, and consequently of society.

Both material and spiritual progress would come about as the result of this self-interest, because, as our more basic and material wants are satisfied, new desires of a higher order constantly form in the human intelligence. It is to satisfy these desires that art, literature, science, and all worthwhile civilized qualities seem to develop.

Frederic Bastiat perceived that, in a society in which all injustice, all force or fraud, were eliminated by giving government a monopoly of force and then by insisting that government must use that monopoly *only* to prevent force, all exchanges in such a society would be free and willing in nature. Since men will not enter a transaction unless they assume themselves bettered by it, in such a free society, the only means by which the individual can pursue his self-interest is by competing most effectively in giving others what they wish to receive from their transactions. Thus, each man furthers his self-interest to the extent that he furthers the interest of the other individuals of society:

> Christianity gave to the world the great principle of the brotherhood of man. It speaks to our hearts, to our sentiments, to our noblest instincts. Political economy proclaims the same principle in the name of cold reason, and, by showing the interrelation of cause and effect, reconciles, in reassuring accord, the calculations of the most wary self-interest with the inspiration of the most sublime morality.

Property

If the ideal of self-interest is to achieve its benefits for society, one vital precondition is the understanding of property and its close connection with human nature:

> Property is a necessary consequence of the nature of man.
>
> In the full sense of the word, man *is born a proprietor,* because he is born with wants whose satisfaction is necessary to life, and with organs and faculties whose exercise is indispensable to the satisfaction of these wants. Faculties are only an extension of the person; and property is nothing but an extension of the faculties. To separate a man from his faculties is to cause him to die; to separate a man from the product of his faculties is likewise to cause him to die.
>
> There are some political theorists who are very much concerned with knowing how God ought to have made man. We, for our part, study man as God has made him. We observe that he cannot live without providing for his wants, that he cannot provide for his wants without labor, and that he will not perform any labor if he is not *sure* of applying the fruit of his labor to the satisfaction of his wants.
>
> That is why we believe that property has been divinely instituted, and that the object of human law is its *protection* or *security.*

Bastiat warned that the social architects tended to base their programs upon the assumption that property came into existence because there were laws, whereas in fact, laws had come into existence because there was property. Thus, property was a right so basic to human nature that it came before political organization:

> It is because of these primordial facts, which are necessary consequences of the very nature of man, that the law intervenes. As the desire for life and self-development can induce the strong man to despoil the weak, and thus to violate his right to the fruits of his labor, it has been agreed that the combined force of all members of society should be devoted to preventing and repressing violence. The function of the law, then, is to safeguard the right to property. It is not property that is a matter of agreement, but law. . . .
>
> Property, the right to enjoy the fruits of one's labor, the right to work, to develop, to exercise one's faculties, according to one's own understanding, without the state intervening otherwise than by its protective action—this is what is meant by liberty.

Liberty

For Bastiat, the words "property" and "liberty" merely expressed two aspects of the same fundamental idea. In his view, liberty was connected with the act of production, while property was connected with the thing produced. In any real sense, one was not possible without the other.

As a defender of liberty, Bastiat was also prepared to defend the word "competition." He pointed out that the many critics of competition were likely to be the same social architects who fancied themselves fit to take over the life and property of the individual. For him, competition was the socially advantageous result stemming from liberty in one's person and property:

Competition is merely the absence of oppression. In things that concern me, I want to make my own choice, and I do not want another to make it for me without regard for my wishes; that is all. And if someone proposes to substitute his judgment for mine in matters that concern me, I shall demand to substitute my judgment for his in matters that concern him. What guarantee is there that this will make things go any better? It is evident that competition is freedom. To destroy freedom of action is to destroy the possibility, and consequently the power, of choosing, of judging, of comparing; it amounts to destroying reason, to destroying thought, to destroying man himself. Whatever their starting point, this is the ultimate conclusion our modern reformers always reach; for the sake of improving society they begin by destroying the individual, on the pretext that all evils come from him, as if all good things did not likewise come from him.

Bastiat saw in competition the ultimate in genuine democracy. He saw competition as an egalitarian device, giving to each man what he most wanted, and bringing within reach of all men the fruits of their production. He pointed out that inequalities came from absence of competition, from political intervention which did not allow men the right to the fruits of their production. Any interference with that process, no matter how well intended, was likely to bear the most severe consequences. Bastiat summarized his entire position:

To tamper with man's freedom is not only to injure him, to degrade him; it is to change his nature, to render him, in so far as such oppression is exercised, incapable of improvement; it is to strip him of his resemblance to the Creator, to stifle within him the noble breath of life with which he was endowed at his creation.

Conservatives and Libertarians

In this ideological age, I suspect that the attempts of this chapter to generalize the nineteenth-century political thought of those who opposed the omnipotent state are likely to please no one. At least the foregoing analysis, with all of its admitted complexities, may have set the problem in its historical perspective. Of course, most people use "libertarian" and "conservative" as interchangeable in meaning. They usually refer to all opponents of big government who share an appreciation of the fact that in today's world the primary threat to the individual is likely to come from government. The libertarian is likely to base his conception of freedom on the idea of "natural right" and to believe that freedom is therefore a universal abstraction, above and beyond all history and tradition. The conservative is more likely to feel that freedom and the institutions which make it possible are inseparable, insisting that the slow growth of civilization must be carefully nurtured lest it come to an untimely end.

Many traditionalist-conservatives talk little about freedom and much about the pursuit of virtue as man's highest goal. Many libertarians of a strongly rationalist strain are likely to respond that virtue is no one's business and that freedom is man's highest goal. Bastiat would, I believe, tell the traditionist-conservative that the pursuit of virtue can occur only in freedom. He would also tell the no-government libertarians that freedom is possible only in a system in which government makes life and property secure. I suspect that Bastiat might have found much of the bickering of our times peculiarly out of place in the face of the enormous enemy to both virtue and freedom that looms before us in the modern state.

Frederic Bastiat clearly drew many of his ideas from the Enlightenment, especially since most of its ideas had been developed in eighteenth-century France. Human perfectability and progress were deeply embedded in his thought. Thus he tended to give tacit acceptance to the idea that somehow a system could be arrived at *a priori.* In that sense he was a child of the French Revolution as surely as Robespierre, Bentham, or any modern-day Liberal.

It is equally true that he distrusted Tocqueville's conservative adherence to aristocracy. His emphasis upon self-interest as a prime mover in society was far more libertarian than conservative in the sense that the words are now used. Bastiat would have placed little faith in politically imposed restraints for "moral" purposes. The high place he assigned international peace in his "harmonious" system was also more libertarian than conservative.

Yet Bastiat had a deep and abiding belief in God as the source of human dignity and was insistent that political guarantees of property and personal safety were necessary for society to exist. Such ideas are not always accepted in some libertarian circles.

In essence, Bastiat's position may be described as a phase in classical liberalism when it shone briefly but brightly, before beginning the decay which liberalism has since suffered. Bastiat represents a phase combining the best of the conservative and libertarian positions at a moment in time before needless divisions between the two camps were allowed to divert attention from the real enemy of human freedom: the all-powerful central planners who would use government to dominate the lives of men. Bastiat built upon his faith in the freely-choosing individual as the cornerstone of a free society.

If Frederic Bastiat were resurrected today and confronted with the choice of labeling himself a conservative or a libertarian, he might reply, "I believe in human freedom because I believe in God as the source of an inviolable individual dignity. I recognize the necessity for government to protect the life and property of the individual, thus making him truly free. As for the label for my ideas, what difference does it make how we

label the truth—it is still true!" Having thus defined his principles, he would waste no more energy on the matter, preferring,
I am sure, to bend his every energy to striking down the error
he saw around him on every hand in our society, while actively
propagating his faith in free men.

Surely if the modern history of the Western world proves
nothing else, it should at least make abundantly clear how
disastrous can be quests for "human freedom" or quests to
"conserve human values," when they are guided by men who
have lost their bearings. All too often those who would be free
men have only added to their chains, while those who would
conserve the best of human values have found themselves the
agents for the destruction of those values.

When we examine the uncertain and confused history of
those who have defended such causes during the past 200 years,
with all the wrong turnings and failures in the Western world's
struggle for freedom, the importance of Frederic Bastiat's simple testimony of faith in free men takes on new importance.

If "liberalism" can become so totally corrupted, if "conservatism" can sometimes become a mask for political adventurism, if "libertarianism" can occasionally be converted into an
appeal for license in place of freedom, how vastly important it
becomes to make Bastiat's central idea a new rallying point for
the mid-twentieth century: *faith in free men.*

CHAPTER 10

Frederic Bastiat Today

> We see, then, that in almost all of the important actions of life
> we must respect men's free will, defer to their own good judg-
> ment, to that inner light that God has given them to use, and
> beyond this to let the law of responsibility take its course.

THERE ARE A NUMBER OF AREAS IN WHICH WE CAN STILL
learn a great deal from Bastiat, in both economic and political
terms. In economics, Bastiat made a number of telling points
which have direct application in contemporary debate.

The Seen and the Unseen

One of these areas is Bastiat's consistent emphasis upon "the
seen and the unseen." Here, in a brilliant flash of insight,
Bastiat put his finger upon one of the prime fallacies in economic thinking which still haunts the modern world:

> In the economic sphere an act, a habit, an institution, a law produces
> not only one effect, but a series of effects. Of these effects, the first
> alone is immediate; it appears simultaneously with its cause; *it is seen.*
> The other effects emerge only subsequently; *they are not seen;* we are
> fortunate if we *foresee* them.
>
> There is only one difference between a bad economist and a good one:
> the bad economist confines himself to the *visible* effect; the good

economist takes into account both the effect that can be seen and those effects that must be *foreseen.*

Yet this difference is tremendous; for it almost always happens that when the immediate consequence is favorable, the later consequences are disastrous, and vice versa. Whence it follows that the bad economist pursues a small present good that will be followed by a great evil to come, while the good economist pursues a great good to come, at the risk of a small present evil.

Does government spending stimulate the economy? The effects which are seen would seem to prove that it does. But the effect which is not seen is that government cannot spend money which it does not take from the taxpayer in one form or another. As the result, what is not seen is that government can only give to people a portion of what it has already taken from them. What productive miracles might have been wrought had government taxation and inflation not distorted the picture? With the help of such excellent works as Henry Hazlitt's *Economics in One Lesson,* we will find the quality of our economic thinking much improved if we continually recall Bastiat's insistence upon that aspect of economics which lies beneath the surface of man's affairs.

We Are All Consumers

It is said that four days before Bastiat's death, with his mind still racing to record every possible insight which he could discover, he advised future economists, ". . . to treat economic questions always from the consumer's point of view, for the interest of the consumer is identical with that of mankind." Bastiat felt that the most severe errors in economic thinking stem from a failure to recognize that consumption is the end and final cause of all economic phenomena. He pointed out that the consumer becomes richer in proportion as he buys more cheaply, that he buys more cheaply as goods become more abundant, and that abundance is produced by allowing the fullest possible production. Thus all laws designed to interfere with the productive miracle are eventually laws punishing the consumer. Stressing the enormous interdependence of all men in the market place, emphasizing the fact that the farmer does not make his own clothes, the tailor does not raise the wheat which he consumes, and so on for the countless other benefits which we all daily derive from the market place, Bastiat insisted that the enormous saving in time and effort which came about from division of labor and free exchange provided a system in which the more effective producer was the strongest possible ally of the consumer. He pointed out that the man who profited from the low cost and ready availability of a product was the man who consumed it. Attempts to interfere with that relationship would inevitably prove to be defeating for society as a whole:

> If you wish to prosper, let your customer prosper. This is a lesson it has taken you a very long time to learn.
>
> When people have learned this lesson, everyone will seek his individual welfare in the general welfare. Then jealousies between man and man, city and city, province and province, nation and nation, will no longer trouble the world.

Production of True Wealth

Asking the rhetorical question, "Which is preferable for man and for society, abundance or scarcity?" Bastiat stressed a point which modern society still does not understand: "Wealth consists in an abundance of commodities." When we persist in regulating the number of competitors which can enter the market place, limiting the number of hours that a man may work, manipulating the wages and prices which may be charged, we demonstrate our absurd belief that limiting men's freedom to produce and compete will somehow make us all wealthier. Of course, every limitation exacts its toll from the market place, and ultimately from each consumer. There is no difference in principle between a tariff, a regulatory commission, or any other variety of present-day interventionism, and Bastiat's facetious suggestion that candlemakers and their allied industries should receive government protection against the unfair competition of the sun. With Bastiat, we might ask:

> . . . are we to believe that the people are better fed under the laws that prevail at present, because there is *less* bread, meat, and sugar in the country? Are they better clad, because there is *less* linen and woolen cloth? Are their houses better heated, because there is *less* coal? Is their labor made easier, because there is *less* iron and copper, or because there are *fewer* tools and machines? . . .
>
> Restrictive laws always present us with the same dilemma.
>
> Either we admit that they produce scarcity, or we do not admit it.
>
> If we do admit it, we thereby confess that they inflict upon the people all the harm that they can do. If we do not admit it, then we deny that they limit the supply of goods and raise their prices, and consequently we deny that they favor the producer.
>
> Such laws are either injurious or ineffective. They cannot be useful.

The Necessity of Capital

In an age when capital and labor were assumed to be antagonistic, Bastiat pointed out that capital and labor cannot get along without each other. He urged the freest and most voluntary transactions between capital and labor, and warned that any intervention on behalf of one against the other was likely to produce results which would penalize all.

Bastiat insisted that absolute poverty had been the starting point for mankind, and that the only possible road upward from general poverty was through the formation of capital, of savings put to productive use, savings making the skills of the individual worker far more productive than they would otherwise be.

Speaking to an age almost as blind to this relationship as our own, Bastiat warned the French worker:

> The questions for the worker to ask himself are not: Does my labor bring me a great deal? Does it bring me very little? Does it bring me as much as it brings another? Does it bring me what I should like?
>
> Rather, he should ask: Does my labor bring me less because I have put it at the service of the capitalist? Would it bring me more if I performed it on my own, or if I joined my labor with that of others as destitute as I am? My situation is bad. Would I be better off if there were no capital on earth? If the share that I receive as a result of my arrangement with capital is larger than my share would be without it, what grounds do I have for complaint? And then, if transactions are free and voluntary, what are the laws determining whether there is to be a rise or a fall in the amount of our respective shares? If the nature of these transactions is such that, as the total to be distributed increases, my share in the increase becomes steadily larger, then, instead of vowing eternal hatred against the capitalist, ought I not to look upon him as a good brother? If it is well established that the presence of capital is advantageous to me, and that its absence would mean my death, am I very wise or prudent in abusing it, intimidating it, requiring it to be frittered away or forcing it into hiding?

If fishermen would prefer to fish without the boats and nets which belong to another, or if workers would prefer to work without the machines which belong to a capitalist, let them do so. When the situation is phrased in this way, it demonstrates the utter absurdity of anti-capitalist political interventions, interventions presumably designed to aid the workers.

The truly democratic feature of the new industrial order rested partially upon the greatly increased production which modern capitalism made possible. As more and more goods were produced, Bastiat pointed out that the tendency of that production was to drive prices down and still further down, rendering more and more material goods available to the workers and to the "common people" of society. Another truly democratic impulse stemming from modern capitalism was precisely that men had available to them the opportunity to emerge from the status of wage earners to become capitalists themselves. The idea of savings, and the idea of the individual property right implicit in the investment of those savings, were for Bastiat the realization of the middle-class dream whereby all men in society would come to share an increasingly improved material existence. His speculations of well over a century ago have been amply demonstrated in the society of our times. Bastiat foresaw the enormous middle-class structure of present society. He foresaw the vast prosperity which could accompany a society based upon individual production and the ideal of private property. He did not foresee that we, even after such a convincing demonstration of how well freedom performs its task, would persist in political interventions which work against everything that serves as the basis for our prosperity.

Political Solutions

Frederic Bastiat lived through turbulent times, including three major revolutions and their inevitable traveling companions, anarchy and dictatorship. More important, he lived through all the failures of human society and individual character which so plague the modern world. Only when we fully understand his times can we fully appreciate his political insight. In our own era, in a nation composed almost entirely of one enormous middle class, it is not surprising that middle-class democracy has a strong appeal. Of course, when things now go wrong, it is awkward to have no aristocracy to use as a scapegoat, as the middle classes did in Bastiat's time. Still, mid-nineteenth-century France and our own era have much in common in political terms. It is true that the middle class constitutes a higher percentage of present-day American society, but the essential point is that in both societies the middle classes have assumed that placing all power in their hands would provide the solution of society's problems. The resultant "middle-class democracy" is now commonplace throughout the Western world, and has repeatedly borne bitter fruit. Bastiat had already learned that lesson well between 1830 and 1848.

Economic Decisions at the Ballot Box

Economic decisions made by way of the ballot box can only have one possible outcome: an attempt to "equalize prosperity." Bastiat warned that, no matter how benevolent and generous the original intention, the underlying principle is so vicious that the end result will always be an equalization, but an equalization of poverty, not prosperity. The more schemes, the more arrangements, the more interventions in free exchange, the greater the distortions which will occur, rendering society poorer on net balance.

Viewing the blind democratic staggers of France during the first half of the nineteenth century, Bastiat predicted that the

failure of intervention would in no wise reduce the lust for
further interventions:

> ... each of us, more or less, would like to profit from the labor of
> others. One does not dare to proclaim this feeling publicly, one
> conceals it from oneself, and then what does one do? One imagines
> an intermediary; one addresses the *state,* and each class proceeds
> in turn to say to it: "You, who can take fairly and honorably, take
> from the public and share with us." Alas! The state is only too
> ready to follow such diabolical advice; for it is composed of cabi-
> net ministers, of bureaucrats, of men, in short, who, like all men,
> carry in their hearts the desire, and always enthusiastically seize
> the opportunity, to see their wealth and influence grow. The state
> understands, then, very quickly the use it can make of the role the
> public entrusts to it. It will be the arbiter, the master, of all desti-
> nies. It will take a great deal; hence, a great deal will remain for
> itself. It will multiply the number of its agents; it will enlarge the
> scope of its prerogatives; it will end by acquiring overwhelming
> proportions.

Such a growth of political intervention is sure to reduce
individual initiative. Once the intervention of the state is sufficiently massive, all initiative is stifled:

> ... when ... we permit the makers of utopias to impose their schemes
> on us ... , who does not see that all the foresight and prudence that
> Nature has implanted in the heart of man is turned against industrial
> progress?

> Where, at such a time, is the bond speculator who would dare set
> up a factory or engage in an enterprise? Yesterday it was decreed
> that he will be permitted to work only for a fixed number of
> hours. Today it is decreed that the wages of a certain type of labor
> will be fixed. Who can foresee tomorrow's decree, that of the day
> after tomorrow, or those of the days following? Once the legislator
> is placed at this incommensurable distance from other men, and
> believes, in all conscience, that he can dispose of their time, their
> labor, and their transactions, all of which are their *property,* what

man in the whole country has the least knowledge of the position in which the law will forcibly place him and his line of work tomorrow? And, under such conditions, who can or will undertake anything?

It is for this reason that public service nearly always eliminates competing private services. What private agency can operate effectively against a competitor completely freed from all considerations of cost? Of course, government usually takes the accompanying step of securing a perfect monopoly position by means of a law rendering its competition illegal.

The punishing price involved in the expansion of the public sector rests ultimately upon the individual citizen:

When the satisfaction of a want becomes the object of a public service, it is in large part removed from the sphere of individual freedom and responsibility. The individual is no longer free to buy what he wishes, when he wishes, to consult his means, his convenience, his situation, his tastes, his moral standards, any more than he can determine the relative order in which it seems reasonable to him to provide for his wants. Willy-nilly, he must accept from society, not the amount of service that he deems useful, as he does with private services, but the amount that the government has seen fit to prepare for him, whatever be its quantity and quality. Perhaps he does not have enough bread to satisfy his hunger, and yet the government takes from him a part of his bread, which would be indispensable to him, in order to give him instruction or public spectacles that he neither needs nor desires. He ceases to exercise free control over the satisfaction of his own wants, and, no longer having any responsibility for satisfying them, he naturally ceases to concern himself with doing so. Foresight becomes as useless to him as experience. He becomes less his own master; he has lost, to some extent, his free will; he has less initiative for self-improvement; he is less of a man. Not only does he no longer judge for himself in a given case, but he loses the habit of judging for himself. This moral torpor, which takes possession of him, likewise takes possession of his fellow citizens, and we have seen entire nations fall in this way into disastrous inertia.

Social Decisions at the Ballot Box

In his struggle to free economic decisions from the ballot box, Bastiat was faced with the charge that he lacked "social conscience":

> But, by an inference as false as it is unjust, when we oppose subsidies, we are charged with opposing the very thing that it was proposed to subsidize and of being the enemies of all kinds of activity, because we want these activities to be voluntary and to seek their proper reward in themselves. Thus, if we ask that the state not intervene, by taxation, in religious matters, we are atheists. If we ask that the state not intervene, by taxation, in education, then we hate enlightenment. If we say that the state should not give, by taxation, an artificial value to land or to some branch of industry, then we are the enemies of property and of labor. If we think that the state should not subsidize artists, we are barbarians who judge the arts useless.

> I protest with all my power against these inferences. Far from entertaining the absurd thought of abolishing religion, education, property, labor, and the arts when we ask the state to protect the free development of all these types of human activity without keeping them on the payroll at one another's expense, we believe, on the contrary, that all these vital forces of society should develop harmoniously under the influence of liberty and that none of them should become, as we see has happened today, a source of trouble, abuses, tyranny, and disorder.

> Our adversaries believe that an activity that is neither subsidized nor regulated is abolished. We believe the contrary. Their faith is in the legislator, not in mankind. Ours is in mankind, not in the legislator.

Thus Bastiat struggled unceasingly against those who would regulate the lives of all men. The fact that the regulation of one man by another was filtered through the intermediary of the state in no wise lessened the moral culpability involved. The basic immorality involved in coercion of men soon corrupts not only the wielder of such power, but those over whom the power is wielded. Soon all men come to expect that their lives should be rendered problem-free by an omnicompetent state. For this reason, Bastiat described the state as *"that great fictitious entity by which everyone seeks to live at the expense of everyone else."*

Bastiat realized that the original sin in this regard had stemmed from the upper classes, who for so many centuries had been willing to use political power to maintain their privileges. But he perceived almost immediately that the acquisition of political power by the middle class would only compound and not solve the problem. Soon the middle classes were using that political power to bestow privileges upon themselves. Not too surprisingly, the lower classes resented the middle-class barbecue, and insisted upon joining in the privileges. The Revolution of 1848 was the result of their insistence. In twentieth-century democracy, we have eliminated the class aspect of the problem, by moving almost all Americans into the great middle class, but we are still endeavoring to live at the expense of one another.

Education as Propaganda

Another fundamental conflict which Bastiat saw between the protestations and the actions of the social planners centered upon viewing men as incompetent to make their own decisions, yet presuming at the next moment that these same men were capable of deciding the course of society by means of universal suffrage. Either men are competent to make their own decisions or they are not, but the social planners must no longer be allowed to court political power by giving with one hand and taking away with the other.

Bastiat saw in compulsory, publicly-financed education the means by which the social architects could mold society to their will, thus being safe to advocate universal suffrage, since they were sure that the men so molded would clamour for a society centrally planned and controlled:

> And why do political parties aspire to take over the direction of education? Because they know the saying of Leibnitz: "Make me the master of education, and I will undertake to change the world." Education by governmental power, then, is education by a political party, by a sect momentarily triumphant; it is education on behalf of one idea, of one system, to the exclusion of all others.

So long as taxes were collected by force to subsidize a public educational system, Bastiat understood that no genuine freedom of choice was present for the parent in the education of his own children. He well understood that few parents could carry the double burden of providing for the private education of their children in addition to the educational taxes, and, as the result, the state and its capacities for manipulation and indoctrination would play an ever larger role in the education of future citizens. Thus a vicious circle was in operation:

> From year to year, by means of universal suffrage, national opinion will be embodied in the magistrates, and then the magistrates will mold national opinion as they like . . .

> To pervert the human mind—that is the problem which seems to have been posed and which has been solved by those to whom the monopoly of eduction has been handed over.

The Limitations of Political Solutions

Frederic Bastiat constantly returned to the theme that personal responsibility was an absolute prerequisite for dignity or free-

dom of any kind. Once the community has the right to decide
everything and to regulate everything, the will of the individual
is replaced by the will of the lawmaker and the social architect.
The resultant system closely parallels the relationship between
a flock of sheep and its shepherd.Government is force and force
can be used legitimately only in safeguarding liberty. Any extension of force beyond that point, since it produces disruptions
of individual responsibility, is likely also to produce the destruction of society as a whole. In short, those who are truly
concerned about the maintenance of social order, will attempt
a reduction of governmental authority, since it is intervention
which is the underlying cause of social disorder. Bastiat provides us with excellent advice for our own times:

> There are those who believe that a government whose authority is
> strictly circumscribed is the weaker on that account. It appears to
> them that numerous functions and numerous agencies give the state
> the stability of a broader base. But this is purely an illusion. If the state
> cannot go beyond certain definitely established limits without becom-
> ing an instrument of injustice, ruination, and plunder, without upset-
> ting the natural distribution of industry, satisfactions, capital, and
> manpower, without creating potent causes of unemployment, indus-
> trial crises, and poverty, without increasing crime, without having
> recourse to ever more stringent repressive measures, without stirring
> up discontent and resentment, how will it derive any guarantee of
> stability from these accumulated elements of civil disorder?
>
> . . . it seems evident to me that to restrict the public police force to
> its one and only rightful function, but a function that is essential,
> unchallenged, constructive, desired and accepted by all, is the way to
> win its universal respect and co-operation. Once this is accomplished,
> I cannot see from what source could come all our present ills of
> systematic obstructionism, parliamentary bickering, street insurrec-
> tions, revolutions, crises, factions, wild notions, demands advanced by
> all men to govern under all possible forms, new systems, as dangerous
> as they are absurd, which teach the people to look to the government

for everything. We should have an end also to . . . crushing and inevitably inequitable taxation, to the ever increasing and unnatural meddling of politics in all things, and to that large-scale and wholly artificial redistribution of capital and labor which is the source of needless irritation, of constant ups and downs, of economic crises and setbacks. All these and a thousand other causes of disturbances, friction, disaffection, envy, and disorder would no longer exist; and those entrusted with the responsibility of governing would work together for, and not against, the universal harmony.

Bastiat had lived through monarchy, middle-class democracy, and egalitarian democracy, each punctuated with periodical revolution. In his last days, he correctly predicted the imminent rise of dictatorship. Thus he experienced the full spectrum of political events. His genius rests on the fact that he recognized the impossibility of any lasting political solution, no matter who might control the state, so long as we fail to appreciate the necessity for individual freedom and for strict limitation of political authority to the task of protecting life and poverty.

Individual Choice and Individual Responsibility

For Bastiat, the essence of social organization rested in a single idea:

> We see, then, that in almost all of the important actions of life we must respect men's free will, defer to their own good judgment, to that inner light that God has given them to use, and beyond this to let the law of responsibility take its course.

He knew that human transactions were not possible in any lasting way without barter, exchange, appraisal, and value, and he knew that none of these acts of choice were possible without freedom, nor was freedom possible without responsibility. Bastiat's solution was simply stated in the phrase, "freedom of transactions":

> God has endowed mankind also with all that it needs to accomplish its destiny. There is a providential social physiology, as there is a providential individual physiology. Social organs too are so constituted as to develop harmoniously in the open air of liberty. Away, then, with the quacks and the planners! Away with their rings, their chains, their hooks, their pincers! Away with their artificial methods! Away with their social workshop, their phalanstery, their statism, their centralization, their tariffs, their universities, their state religion, their interest-free credit or bank monopolies, their regulations, their restrictions, their moralization, and their equalization by taxation! And after vainly inflicting so many systems on the body politic, let us end where we should have begun. Let us cast out all artificial systems and give freedom a chance—freedom, which is an act of faith in God and in His handiwork.

Bastiat's Advice for Tomorrow

Frederic Bastiat had some specific advice for us concerning the means by which the admirable goal of freedom might be attained. One valuable bit of advice was his insistence upon a proper method in dealing with the social architects and all others who would undercut individual freedom. Bastiat possessed wit, charm, and a powerful logic on a level far beyond most of us, but he did make it clear how we all might utilize some of the same techniques which he rendered so exquisitely. If there ever was such a thing as a "happy libertarian" that man was Frederic Bastiat. He was fond of poking fun at the pomposities of the social planner. He could use exaggeration to make a telling point. As Henry Hazlitt has pointed out in his introduction to one of Bastiat's books:

He was the master of the *reductio ad absurdum*. Someone suggests that the proposed new railroad from Paris to Madrid should have a break at Bordeaux. The argument is that if goods and passengers are forced to stop at that city, it will be profitable for boatmen, porters, hotelkeepers and others there. Good, says Bastiat. But then why not break it also at Angouleme, Poitiers, Tours, Orleans, and, in fact, at all intermediate points? The more breaks there are, the greater the amount paid for storage, porters, extra cartage. We could have a railroad consisting of nothing but such gaps—a negative railroad!

Another favorite tool of Bastiat was repetition. He knew that points must be reduced to their simplest terms, and then stated and restated in different forms to drive the message home. Sometimes the opponents of big government feel that once they have made a case, the subject needs no further comment. They forget how the same statist fallacies will rise again and again in different forms.

In Bastiat's insistence upon a sense of humor and upon frequent repetition of basic principles, using a variety of engaging illustrations, he makes clear what so many of us forget: No amount of political activity or electioneering will ever establish the idea of human freedom *until* the idea has taken possession of the minds of men. It is in the field of education, and not the field of politics, that the primary battle must be fought and won.

In another of his brilliant observations, Bastiat also put his finger upon one of the hopeful signs we might observe in the situation which we face in the twentieth century. He perceived that socialism was inevitably its own worst enemy, and would eventually destroy itself. He felt assured that the fundamental values involved in family, property, justice, and freedom were so deeply engraved in the minds and hearts of men that they would one day emerge in reaction against the chaotic failures of socialism. Bastiat thus possessed a faith that "freedom works." He believed that no amount of propaganda could indefinitely keep that fact a secret from the men who compose society. Such a fundamental faith is more needed today than ever before.

We could use more Bastiats today. Such men are hard to define and hard to locate. Perhaps this is true because the Bastiats of this world are always "a man alone." Bastiat was "a man alone" not only in his personal life, but in the face of the intellectual currents of his times. Probably any modern-day Bastiats would be equally off the beaten path.

If we discover any modern counterpart of Frederic Bastiat, he is likely to be his own man. He is likely to advise the conservatives and libertarians of twentieth-century America that they should scrupulously avoid labels, concentrating not on ideology, but on the obviously pressing problem of bringing human freedom once again into a central position in the minds and hearts of all men.

The sweeping changes of the Industrial Revolution, coupled with the equally sweeping changes of popular democratic politics, inevitably brought with them a new society. Bastiat was far more able than conservatives like Burke and Tocqueville to come to terms with that new society, but, unlike the rationalists (from which liberalism and certain strains of libertarianism are sprung), he did not make *Freedom* and *Man* into abstractions. He insisted that men were imperfect and unique, that freedom could be found only by protecting the individual's life, liberty, and property from the predations of other men, organized or unorganized. Thus he adapted a unique conservative-libertarian position, well-suited to a difficult transitional stage in modern history.

In that unique middle way between the conservative and

the libertarian, Bastiat offers us a great deal. It is true that the twentieth century has brought special concerns such as the Cold War, the problems of modern technology, and the mythic erosion of American life which today leaves us a people unsure of who and what we are. For these unique problems, we must find our own unique solutions. What Bastiat has done is light the way to a path which we must now discover for ourselves.

This is the heritage of Frederic Bastiat, "the man alone."

Aphorisms

FREDERIC BASTIAT IS AMONG THE MOST QUOTABLE OF AU-
thors. Samples of his wit, clarity, and penetration brighten the
preceding pages. Of course, no brief quotation does justice to
any author with a significant message. Bastiat should be read
in full. Fortunately for our later generation, much of Bastiat's
work is available in a moderately-priced and well-made new
edition. The Foundation for Economic Education, Irvington-
on-Hudson, New York, has recently re-issued *Economic Harmonies, Economic Sophisms,* and *Selected Essays on Political
Economy,* containing "the best of Bastiat."

Since Bastiat's work contains so much of value for an understanding of our own times, it seems fitting to conclude this
study of his life with some of his aphorisms—a legacy to latter-
day believers in freedom. No quotation used in the text is here
repeated. All quotations appear in the latest editions of *Harmonies, Sophisms,* and *Selected Essays* described above.

Bastiat's insight, and his sense of humor, should help us to
face the difficult task of education which lies ahead:

Politics

The proper domain of law and governments is justice.

***

But the individual has no right to use force for any other end. I
cannot legitimately *force* my fellow men to be industrious, sober,

thrifty, generous, learned, or pious; but I can force them to be just.

For the same reason, the collective force cannot be legitimately employed to foster the love of labor, sobriety, thrift, generosity, learning, religious faith; but it can be legitimately employed to further the rule of justice, to defend every man's rights.

**

Within the limits of equity, everything is to be accomplished through the free and perfectible initiative of man; nothing is to be achieved by law or by force save universal justice.

**

Try to imagine a system of labor imposed by force that is not a violation of liberty; a transfer of wealth imposed by force that is not a violation of property rights. If you cannot do so, then you must agree that the law cannot organize labor and industry without organizing injustice.

**

Unhappy country, where the sacred forces that were meant to support each man's rights are perverted to accomplish themselves the violation of these rights!

**

Shall I speak of the corrupting immorality that seeps into the veins of the whole body politic when, in principle, the law puts itself at the service of every spoliative impulse? Attend a meeting of the National Assembly when bonuses, subsidies, bounties, restrictions are on the agenda. See with what shameless rapacity everyone tries to make sure of his share of the plunder—plunder to which he would blush to stoop as a private individual.

**

The ideological war now being waged against property is neither the most bitter nor the most dangerous that it has had to contend with. Since the beginning of the world there has also been a real war of violence and conspiracy waged against it that gives no sign of abating. War, slavery, imposture, inequitable taxation, monopoly, privilege, unethical practices, colonialism, the right to employment, the right to credit, the right to education, the right to public aid, progressive taxation in direct or inverse ratio to the ability to pay—all are so many battering rams pounding against the tottering column. Could anyone assure me whether there are many men in France, even among those who consider themselves conservatives, who do not, in one form or another, lend a hand to this work of destruction?

***

How could men dream of blaming themselves for their woes when they have been persuaded that by nature they are inert, that the source of all action, and consequently of all responsibility, lies outside themselves, in the will of the sovereign and of the lawgiver?

***

Certain nations seem particularly liable to fall prey to governmental plunder. They are those in which men, lacking faith in their own dignity and capability, would feel themselves lost if they were not *governed and administered* every step of the way. Without having traveled a great deal, I have seen countries in which the people think that agriculture can make no progress unless the government supports experimental farms; that soon there will no longer be any horses, if the government does not provide studs; that fathers will not have their children educated, or will have them taught only immorality, if the government does not decide what it is proper to learn.

***

People are beginning to realize that the apparatus of government is costly. But what they do not know is that the burden falls *inevitably* on them.

***

The truth is, the word "gratuitous" as applied to public services contains the grossest, and, I may add, the most childish of fallacies. I marvel at the public's extreme gullibility in being taken in by this word. People ask us, "Are you against *gratuitous* education? *Gratuitous* stud farms?

Quite the contrary! I'm for them and I would also be for gratuitous food and gratuitous housing. . . . if these were possible.

***

When a nation is burdened with taxes, nothing is more difficult, as I would say, impossible, than to levy them equally. The statisticians and fiscal authorities no longer even try to do so. What is still more difficult, however, is to shift the tax burden onto the shoulders of the rich. The state can have an abundance of money only by taking from everyone and especially from the masses.

***

In a country where no law may be voted and no tax may be levied save with the consent of those whom the law is to govern and upon whom the tax is to fall, the public can be robbed only if it is first deceived. Our ignorance is the *raw material* of every extortion that is practiced upon us, and we may be certain beforehand that every *sophism* is the precursor of an act of plunder. My friends, when you detect a sophism in a petition, get a good grip on your wallet, for you may be sure that this is what the petitioners are aiming at.

***

But what is most noteworthy is the astonishing blindness of the public to all this. When victorious soldiers reduced the vanquished to slavery, they were barbarous, but they were not absurd. Their object was, as ours is, to live at the expense of others but, unlike us, they attained it. What are we to think of a people who apparently do not suspect that *reciprocal pillage* is no less pillage because it is reciprocal; that it is no less criminal because it is carried out legally and in an orderly manner; that it adds nothing to the public welfare; that, on the contrary, it diminishes it by all that this spendthrift intermediary that we call the *state* costs?

***

In the realm of government operation it may happen that functionaries receive services from the citizens without rendering services in return; in that case the taxpayer suffers a loss, no matter what illusion the circulation of bank notes may create.

***

. . . the state has no resources of its own. It has nothing, it possesses nothing that it does not take from the workers. When, then, it meddles in everything, it substitutes the deplorable and costly activity of its own agents for private activity.

***

. . . we must wait until we have learned by experience—perhaps cruel experience—to trust in the state a little less and in mankind a little more.

***

. . . *heavy government expenditures* and *liberty* are incompatible.

***

. . . the government offers to cure all the ills of mankind. It promises to restore commerce, make agriculture prosperous, expand industry, encourage arts and letters, wipe out poverty, etc., etc. All that is needed is to create some new government agencies and to pay a few more bureaucrats.

***

The state too is subject to the Malthusian law. It tends to expand in proportion to its means of existence and to live beyond its means, and these are, in the last analysis, nothing but the substance of the people. Woe to the people that cannot limit the sphere of action of the state! Freedom, private enterprise, wealth, happiness, independence, personal dignity, all vanish.

***

Economics

. . . not to know political economy is to allow oneself to be dazzled by the immediate effect of a phenomenon; to know political economy is to take into account the sum total of all effects, both immediate and future.

***

Good Lord! What a lot of trouble to prove in political economy that two and two make four; and if you succeed in doing so, people cry, "It is so clear that it is boring." Then they vote as if you had never proved anything at all.

***

"In the sweat of thy face shalt thou eat bread." But everyone wants as much bread and as little sweat as possible. History provides conclusive proof of this.

***

. . . certain men have recourse to the law in order to abridge the natural prerogatives of this freedom on the part of other men. This kind of plunder is called privilege or monopoly.

***

Slavery is on its way out, thank Heaven, and our natural inclination to defend our property makes direct and outright plunder difficult. One thing, however, has remained. It is the unfortunate primitive tendency which all men have to divide their complex lot in life into two parts, shifting the pains to others and keeping the satisfactions for themselves.

***

. . . plunder . . . has unleashed on our planet wars, slavery, serfdom, feudalism, the exploitation of public ignorance and credulity, privileges, monopolies, trade restrictions, public loans, commercial frauds, excessive taxes, and, lastly, the war against capital and the absurd demand of everyone to live and to develop at the expense of everyone else.

***

Brotherhood! Sacred tie that joins soul to soul, divine spark come down from heaven into the hearts of men, how can thy name be thus taken in vain? In thy name it is proposed to stifle all freedom. In thy name it is proposed to erect a new despotism such as the world has never seen; and we may well fear that after serving as a protection for so many incompetents, as a cloak for so many ambitious schemers, as a bauble for so many who haughtily scorn human dignity, it will at last, discredited and with sullied name, lose its great and noble meaning.

***

This is called . . . brotherhood: "You have produced; I have not; we are comrades; let us share." "You own something; I own nothing; we are brothers; let us share."

***

Let a merchant begin to sell his goods on the principle of brotherly love, and I do not give him even a month before his children will be reduced to beggary.

***

It is indeed a singular thing that people wish to pass laws to nullify the disagreeable consequences that the law of responsibility entails. Will they never realize that they do not eliminate these consequences, but merely pass them along to other people? The result is one injustice the more and one moral lesson the less. . . .

***

The poorest class in civilized countries is far above the poorest class among savage peoples. It has risen so far; why should it not rise even higher?

***

The present level of consumption enjoyed by an honest and industrious working-class family does not surprise us because habit has familiarized us with this strange situation. If, however, we were to compare the standard of living that this family has attained with the one that would be its lot in a hypothetical social order from which competition had been excluded; if statisticians could measure with precision instruments, as with a dynamometer, its labor in relation to its satisfactions at two different periods; we should realize that freedom, despite all still-existing restrictions on it, has wrought a miracle so enduring that for that very reason we fail to be aware of it.

***

We have the distressing and unreasonable habit of attributing to *society* the suffering that we see about us. . . . To be able to assert that even the most unfortunate of men are worse off in society than out of it, we should have to begin by proving that the poorest of our fellow men has to bear, in the social state, a heavier burden of privations and suffering than would have been his lot in solitude. . . . The most impassioned advocate of the *state of nature,* Rousseau himself, admitted that . . . men did without everything . . . ; they went naked, they slept in the open air. Thus, Rousseau himself, in order to present the state of nature favorably, was obliged to make happiness consist in privation. But I affirm that even this negative happiness is a delusion, and that man in the state of isolation would surely die in a very few hours. Perhaps Rousseau would have gone so far as to say that that would be the true perfection. He would have been consistent, for if happiness lies in privation, then perfection lies in annihilation.

***

. . . it is a strange kind of harmony that can be achieved only by an external and despotic act that runs contrary to the interests of all!

***

. . . that marvelous and special gift that God has bestowed upon man: *free will!*

We are endowed with the faculty of comparing, of judging, of choosing, and of acting accordingly. This implies that we can arrive at a good or a bad judgment, make a good or a bad choice—a fact that it is never idle to remind men of when we speak to them of liberty.

***

. . . is it so difficult to permit men to experiment, to feel their way, to choose, to make mistakes, to correct them, to learn, to work together, to manage their own property and their own interests, to act for themselves, at their own risk and peril, on their own responsibility? Do we not see that this is what makes them men? Must we always start with the fatal premise that all those who govern are guardians and all the governed are wards?

***

For my part, it seems to me that there is a connection between the aspiration that impels all men towards the improvement of their material, intellectual, and moral condition, and the faculties with which they are endowed to realize this aspiration.

Hence, I should like each man to have, on his own responsibility, the free disposition, administration, and control of his own person, his acts, his family, his transactions, his associations, his intelligence, his faculties, his labor, his capital, and his property.

***

You say that I would do better to follow a given career, to work in a given way, to use a steel plow instead of a wooden one, to sow sparsely rather than thickly, to buy from the East rather than from the West. I maintain the contrary. I have made my calculations; after all, I am more vitally concerned than you in not making a mistake in matters that will decide my own well-being, the happiness of my family, matters that concern you only as they touch your vanity or your systems. Advise me, but do not force your opinion on me. I shall decide at my *peril and risk;* that is enough, and for the law to interfere would be tyranny.

***

. . . since liberty is still a sacred word and still has the power to stir men's hearts, her enemies would strip her of her name and her prestige and, rechristening her *competition,* would lead her forth to sacrifice while the applauding multitudes extend their hands to receive their chains of slavery.

***

. . . self-interest is that indomitable individualistic force within us that urges us on to progress and discovery, but at the same time disposes us to monopolize our discoveries. Competition is that no less indomitable humanitarian force that wrests progress, as fast as it is made, from the hands of the individual and places it at the disposal of all mankind. These two forces, which may well be deplored when considered individually, work together to create our social harmony.

***

Let men labor, exchange, learn, band together, act, and react upon
one another, since in this way, according to the laws of Providence,
there can result from their free and intelligent activity only order,
harmony, progress, and all things that are good. . . .

***

. . . even as man in his relation to his Creator is raised above the beasts
by his religious feeling, in his dealings with his fellow men by his sense
of justice, in his dealings with himself by his morality, so, in finding
his means of survival and increase, he is distinguished from them by
a remarkable phenomenon, namely, *exchange.*

***

Shall I try to portray the state of poverty, barrenness, and ignorance
in which, without the faculty of exchange, the human species would
have wallowed eternally, if indeed, it would not have disappeared
altogether from the face of the earth?

***

By virtue of exchange, one man's prosperity is beneficial to all others.

***

. . . if coercion assumes endless forms, freedom has only one. Once
again, the free and voluntary transfer of services from one person to
another can be defined in these simple words: Give me this, and I will
give you that. Do this for me, and I will do that for you.

***

In a country like the United States, where the right to property is
placed above the law, where the sole function of the public police force
is to safeguard this natural right, each person can in full confidence
dedicate his capital and his labor to production. He does not have to
fear that his plans and calculations will be upset from one instant to
another by the legislature.

The Social Architects

And surely one of the saddest sights that can present itself to anyone
who loves mankind is that of a productive age bending all its efforts

to infect itself—by way of education—with the thoughts, the senti-
ments, the errors, the prejudices, and the vices of a nation of plunder-
ers. Our age is often accused of a lack of consistency, of a failure
to show any correlation between the ideals it professes and the
way of life it pursues. The criticism is just, and I believe that
I have here indicated the principal reason why this situation
prevails.

***

. . . the *liberal* party has fallen into the strange contradiction of
disregarding the liberty, the dignity, the perfectibility of man, and of
preferring to them an artificial, stationary, degrading unity, imposed
by turns by all despotic regimes on behalf of the most diverse systems.

***

In all things the guiding principle of these great manipulators of
the human race is to put their own creation in the place of God's
creation. . . .

***

It is true that they are optimists in regard to the future. For, although
mankind, in itself incompetent, has been on the wrong track for six
millennia, a prophet has come who has shown men the way to salvation; and if the flock will only be docile enough to follow the shepherd,
he will lead it into the promised land where prosperity may be attained
without effort, and where order, security, and harmony are the easy
reward of improvidence.

All that men have to do is to permit the reformers to change, as
Rousseau said, *their physical and moral constitution.*

***

It is the unfortunate obsession of our age to wish to give pure abstractions a life of their own, to imagine a city apart from the people who
live in it, mankind independently of the individual men who constitute
it, a whole aside from its component parts, collective life without the
individual units that comprise it.

***

Though everlastingly wrangling with one another over the new institutions they would like to establish, they evince a striking unanimity
in their common hatred of existing institutions, and the wage system
most of all; for, if they cannot reach agreement on the social order of
their choice, we must at least give them their due in that they always
see eye to eye in abusing, deploring, slandering, hating, and generating
hatred for anything that actually exists.

***

We have about a dozen reforms in progress at the same time; they
press on one another like the souls of the departed before the gate to
oblivion, and not one enters.

***

Can the human race establish a new basis for property, family, labor,
and exchange every day in the year? Can it risk changing the social
order every morning?

***

This must be said: There are too many "great" men in the world; there
are too many legislators, planners, founders of societies, leaders of
nations, fathers of their country, etc., etc. Too many people place
themselves above mankind in order to guide its footsteps; too many
people make a career of being concerned with mankind.

***

As we have seen, the legislator, according to the ideas of the ancients,
bears the same relation to mankind as the potter does to the clay.
Unfortunately, when this idea prevails, nobody wants to be the
clay, and everyone wants to be the potter.

***

But, sublime writers, kindly deign to remember sometimes that this
clay, this sand, this dungheap, of which you dispose so arbitrarily, is
composed of men, your equals, intelligent and free beings like you,
who have received from God, like you, the power to see, to plan, to
think, and to judge for themselves!

***

I confess that I am one of those who think that the choice, the impulse, should come from below, not from above, from the citizens, not from the legislator; and the contrary doctrine seems to me to lead to the annihilation of liberty and of human dignity.

***

. . . when the law, by the intervention of its necessary agent, force, imposes a system of labor, a method or a subject of education, a faith or a religion, its action on men is no longer negative, but positive. It substitutes the will of the legislator for their own will, the initiative of the legislator for their own initiative. They no longer have to take counsel together, to compare, to foresee; the law does all this for them. Intelligence becomes a useless accessory; they cease to be men; they lose their personality, their liberty, their property.

***

Let us, therefore, not have the presumption to overthrow everything, to regulate everything, to seek to exempt all, men and things alike, from the operation of the laws to which they are naturally subject. Let us be content to leave the world as God made it. Let us not imagine that we, poor scribblers, are anything but more or less accurate observers. Let us not make ourselves ridiculous by proposing to change humanity, as if we stood apart from it and from its errors and shortcomings.

***

If by ill-advised measures you free men from the responsibility of their acts, they could still be taught by theory—but no longer by experience. And I am not certain that instruction that is not reinforced and backed by experience is not more dangerous than ignorance itself. . . .

***

Meanwhile, socialism has carried its folly so far as to announce the end of all the ills of society, though not of all the ills of the individual. It has not yet dared to predict that man will reach the point where suffering, old age, and death will be eliminated.

***

"Highway robbery," the wise men said, "is neither good nor bad in itself; that depends on circumstances. All that needs to be done is to keep things *evenly balanced* and to pay us government officials well for this labor of balancing. Perhaps pillage has been allowed too much latitude; perhaps it has not been allowed enough. Let us see, let us examine, let us balance the account of each worker. To those who do not earn enough, we shall give a little more of the road to exploit. For those who earn too much, we shall reduce the hours, days, or months during which they will be allowed to pillage."

Those who spoke in this way acquired for themselves a great reputation for moderation, prudence, and wisdom. They never failed to rise to the highest offices in the state.

As for those who said: "Let us eliminate every injustice, for there is no such thing as a partial injustice; let us tolerate no *robbery,* for there is no such thing as a *half-robbery* or a *quarter-robbery,*" they were regarded as idle visionaries, tiresome dreamers who kept repeating the same thing over and over again. Besides, the people found their arguments too easy to understand. How can one believe that what is so simple can be true?

***

You would like to be generous and you cannot be so effectively; what I venture to ask of you is that you be just. Keep your fortune, but let me keep mine. Respect my property as I respect yours.

***

The admirers of unity are very numerous, and that is understandable. By a providential decree, we all have faith in our own judgment, and we believe that there is only one right opinion in the world, namely, our own. Therefore we think that the legislator could do no better than to impose it on everyone; and, the better to be on the safe side, we all want to be that legislator.

***

But once the legislator is elected and freed from his campaign promises, oh, then his language changes! The nation returns to passivity, to inertia, to nothingness, and the legislator takes on the character of omnipotence. His the invention, his the direction, his the impulsion, his the organization. Mankind has nothing to do but to let things be done to it; the hour of despotism has arrived.

***

Note that I am not contesting their right to invent social orders, to disseminate their proposals, to advise their adoption, and to experiment with them on themselves, at their own expense and risk; but I do indeed contest their right to impose them on us by law, that is, by the use of the police force and public funds.

***

For what precise and definite object are all the citizens today to be stamped, like the coinage, with the same image? . . . On what basis would they be cast in the same mold? *And who will possess the mold?* A terrible question, which should give us pause. *Who will possess the mold?* . . .

Is it not simpler to break this fatal mold and honestly proclaim freedom?

***

What of the Future?

Every attempt to divert responsibility from its natural course is an attack upon justice, freedom, order, civilization, or progress.

***

Where are we going? The Assembly must direct itself by some principle; it must commit itself to justice everywhere and for everybody, if it is not, in fact, to rush headlong into the system of legal and reciprocal plunder, to the point of completely equalizing all classes, that is, to the point of communism.

***

. . . gentlemen, organize industry as much as you please. But we, for our part, will take care to see that you do not organize *robbery*.

***

It is not, as people think, the monopolists, but the monopolized, that sustain the monopolies.

***

When misguided public opinion honors what is despicable and despises what is honorable, punishes virtue and rewards vice, encourages what is harmful and discourages what is useful, applauds falsehood and smothers truth under indifference or insult, a nation turns its back on progress and can be restored only by the terrible lessons of catastrophe.

***

Enslavement of the mind! What a frightful association of words! O liberty! We have seen thee hunted from country to country, crushed by conquest, nigh unto death in servitude, jeered at in the courts of the mighty, driven from the schools, mocked in the drawing room, misinterpreted in the studio, anathematized in the temple. It would seem that in thought thou shouldst find an inviolable refuge. But if thou shouldst surrender in this last haven, what becomes of the hope of the ages and of the dignity of man?

***

When education has sown a fatal seed in the soil of public opinion, there is in the body politic a force of self-preservation, *vis medicatrix,* that enables it to rid itself, at long last, after many sufferings and tears, of the baneful germ with which it has become infected.

***

. . . it takes time for enlightenment to be produced and propagated, and that, in so far as enlightenment is achieved, right no longer needs to be maintained by might, and society regains possession of itself.

***

Young men, in these times when a lamentable skepticism appears to be the effect and the punishment of our intellectual anarchy, I should deem myself happy if the reading of this book would stir you to utter those reassuring words, so sweet to the lips, which are not only a refuge from despair but a positive force, strong enough, we are told, to remove mountains, those words that begin the Christian's profession of faith: *I believe.*

***

The solution of the social problem lies in liberty.

***

What is freedom? It is the sum total of all our freedoms. To be free, on one's own responsibility, to think and to act, to speak and to write, to labor and to exchange, to teach and to learn—this alone is to be free.

***

It can further be affirmed that thanks to the nonintervention of the state in private affairs, wants and satisfactions would develop in their natural order. We should not see poor families seeking instruction in literature before they have bread. We should not see the city being populated at the expense of the country, or the country at the expense of the city. We should not see those great displacements of capital, of labor, and of population which are provoked by legislative measures, displacements that render the very sources of existence so uncertain and precarious, and thereby add so greatly to the responsibilities of the government.

***

I have not made an alliance with anyone; I have not joined either side. On each question, I have voted according to my own conscience.

Index*

* Prepared by Vernelia A. Crawford

References to chapters and parts of chapters under the appropriate subject classification are hyphenated. The number in each other instance refers to the *first* page of a discussion.